Husbands at home

Husbands at home

The domestic economy in a
post-industrial society

Jane Wheelock

Routledge
London and New York

First published in 1990
by Routledge
11 New Fetter Lane, London EC4P 4EE

Simultaneously published in the USA and Canada
by Routledge
a division of Routledge, Chapman and Hall, Inc.
29 West 35th Street, New York, NY 10001

Laserset by LaserScript Ltd, Mitcham, Surrey
Printed and bound in Great Britain by
Biddles Ltd, Guildford and King's Lynn

British Library Cataloguing in Publication Data

Wheelock, Jane, *1944–*
   Husbands at home: the domestic economy in a post-industrial society.
   1. Domestic economy. Economic and social aspects
   305.9′649

Library of Congress Cataloging in Publication Data

Wheelock, Jane, 1944–
   Husbands at home : the domestic economy in a post-industrial
   society / Jane Wheelock.
   p. cm.
   Bibliography: p.
   1. Sexual division of labor—England, Northern—Case studies. 2. Home
economics—England, Northern—Case studies.
   3. Househusbands—England, Northern—Case studies.
   4. Unemployed—England, Northern—Case studies.
   5. Households—England, Northern—Case studies. I. Title.
   HD6060.65.G72E59 1990   89-10403
   305.33′649—dc20   CIP

ISBN 0-415-04669-6

'I think from the old days ... a lot of people have the image of the North East as Andy Capp. The man was the boss. It's changed now. The men have thought, we've got to muck in and do our bit.'

'I'm in the house all day and I'm no going to sit on top of muck, I'm no going to neglect my bairns.'

Contents

Contents

Illustrations

Acknowledgements

Many people have helped me in the process of writing this book. I would like to thank the Equal Opportunities Commission for the grant they gave me to undertake the empirical research, and Sunderland Polytechnic for the time to conduct it. Thanks also to John Stevens and Mavis Morris for providing the link with the Employment Potential in Sunderland project. Kath Price was an invaluable research collaborator, who provided support and friendship through a cold winter of interviews and many spring days spent analysing the tape recordings. Without the unstinting help and co-operation of the Wearside families, of course, none of this would have been possible: I especially want to thank them for their generosity and time.

I have been very grateful for all the help and support that many of my colleagues at Sunderland Polytechnic have given me. Ian Stone, Cherrie Stubbs, and Philip Garrahan in particular have been very encouraging. Jean Davies made very helpful comments on a draft version. Many thanks to Mavis Blenkinsop who gave me the very first interview, and who has continued helping to keep our household running smoothly. It has been wonderful to be able to call on Alex Howard's expertise with the word processor whenever I have needed advice. Thanks finally to Alex, and to my children, Thomas, Jude, and Jessica, for their love and understanding.

Part I

Household Work Strategies in a De-industrialising Economy

The Wearside empirical study

Introduction: the demise of the Andy Capp image of the North East?

The inspiration for this book arose from the unexpected outcome of a study funded by the Equal Opportunities Commission in which working-class Wearside couples were interviewed to find out how the division of domestic work between wives and husbands changed when men became unemployed. There have only been a handful of studies of the effects of unemployment on who does what tasks in the household. Their conclusions have been that male unemployment does little to alter the division of household work, or indeed that it reinforces traditional gender roles within the family.

My study was undertaken in the North East, not merely an area of high unemployment, but one which is often perceived as holding strongly to traditional role stereotypes. Wearside itself represents a particularly stark case of the effects on employment of national and international economic restructuring and de-industrialisation. Whilst employment opportunities for manual workers have declined, the prospects for low-paid women workers have remained relatively buoyant. The couples I chose to interview were representative of this shift in the regional labour market: whilst husbands were out of work, their wives were in either part-time or full-time employment. Amongst the thirty couples interviewed there was a marked shift towards a less traditional division of household work, with men undertaking more domestic work and childcare when they became unemployed. I became interested in trying to establish the links between capital restructuring and the internal dynamics of the household.

There is still much controversy over whether Thatcherite economic policies have been successful in re-establishing prospects for long term economic growth in this country, but it seems likely that a problem of higher regional levels of unemployment will remain with us for some time to come. My empirical work shows that when men leave

3

employment, this has generally precipitated a change in the division of domestic work in a non-traditional direction, though the volume of work undertaken by men is largely determined by the hours that their wives work. In other words, many of the families whom I interviewed had adopted household work strategies which conflicted with traditional views of gender roles. In addition, a substantial minority, where wives worked despite the restrictions of the state benefits system and their own low wages, were also adopting strategies which conflicted with economic rationality. The priority for these households was the self-respect and self-reliance of avoiding dependence on the welfare system. Were there to be a radical and imaginative policy for changing the organisation of work in this country, it would seem that there might be prospects for actively engaging men in housework and childcare, ensuring employment for their wives, and encouraging less stereotyped roles for both sexes.

This book aims to provide both a theoretical and an empirical framework within which such prospects might be considered. On the one hand, structural economic change affects the internal dynamics of the household, in terms of the division of labour between men and women, both in practice and in ideological terms. On the other hand, the way in which households behave, and the work strategies men and women adopt affect the functioning of the labour market and in turn of the economy. The results of my empirical work have led me to question the pessimistic views of sociologists on the prospects for change in gender roles within the household economy. I also query the assumptions that economists make about how households operate, and in particular the view that individual motivations are based on economic rationality.

I am, in other words, concerned to make a contribution both to sociology and to economics, and particularly to the boundaries between these disciplines. Gender has already been extensively integrated into sociology, but there has not been very much work done on incorporating men into gender models. Economics, on the other hand, pays almost no attention to gender issues, and is well known for favouring abstract economic modelling over empirically based enquiry. Whilst my empirical work might be labelled as primarily sociological in context, it has important implications for aspects of economic theory. Economics has generally taken a rigidly separatist line in relation to the other social sciences. I shall be demonstrating that it is only by modifying its assumptions in the light of what other social sciences have learned, and paying some attention to empirical research, that economics will be able to integrate gender into its theoretical concerns. Only then will economics be able to command moral respect.

The book divides into two parts, one theoretically, the other empirically based. The first part includes an analysis of the theoretical themes in recent literature, and provides a framework for linking the internal dynamics of the household economy with the process of global capital restructuring. Chapter 1 sees the household economy as one of the range of productive economic institutions making up total economic activity, and suggests that an institutional model provides a useful analytical tool. The second chapter looks at the employment implications of structural economic change at national and regional levels, and the social recomposition of gender roles this has involved; whilst the third examines recent theoretical models which are of relevance to household work strategies, and the usefulness of the labour process approach is emphasised. In Part II, Chapters 4 and 5 examine empirical work on the domestic economy and the household, focusing on my own results and their implications for the theoretical framework of earlier chapters. Chapter 4 develops a classification system for the gender division of household labour, and then examines the changes in the gender organisation of households brought about by unemployment. The fifth chapter focuses on the subjective effects of unemployment: the strategies men adopt to cope, and the conflict of motivations within the family induced by economic restructuring. It is particularly in Chapter 5 and the Conclusions that the implications of my empirical work for economic theory are drawn out.

Empirical material is presented in both parts of the book in the form of case studies 'Setting the scene' for the chapter which follows. The idea behind setting the scene in this way is to illustrate personal and family aspects of the wider social and economic factors dealt with in each chapter. The intention is not to provide analysis, but to integrate the conceptual and theoretical concerns of the book by introducing relevant empirical material without interfering with the flow of the argument. Each scene-setting is a personal testament to the Wearside families who have shared the way in which their private lives have been affected by the economic events and policies of recent years. It is to a description of this Wearside study that I turn first of all.

The methodology of the Wearside study[1]

My research aimed to test how far the 'double burden' of housework and employment is shared between men and women in times of recession. I wanted to identify the objective and subjective effects of changing patterns of male unemployment on the household: objectively, the extent to which the gender characteristics of work within the household are affected; subjectively, the variations in the attitudes of men and women to the gender relations of housework and childcare on the one hand and to employment on the other. What, in broad terms, are the effects of men no longer being in paid work on the gender basis of family work strategies with respect to housework, childcare, the complementary economy, and formal employment? My approach was informed by the labour process debate, and a concern to extend this to a consideration of work within the household.

Behind these aims lay a concern for policy implications. The thrust of recent policy debate has been directed at the barriers that women face in entering and re-entering the labour force. What are the prospects, in contrast, for actively engaging men in parenthood and housework? Even from a labour market point of view, men's willingness to do housework and childcare means an increase in women's potential for undertaking paid employment. There is also the importance of men's contribution to family life. How deleterious are men's employment experiences to their contribution to the family outside the narrowly economic one of breadwinner? To what extent is unemployment or non-employment an opportunity to ensure family participation amongst men? What policy options might be feasible given present practices and cultural attitudes?

Woman's double burden means a conflict between responsibility towards her family and towards the labour market. Such a conflict is not present for most men (Land 1978). Can domestic and paid work be restructured for both men and women by changing the pattern of employment? For example, a radical shortening of the working week, combined with the extension of parental leave to both parents, has been suggested as a policy both for dealing with unemployment and for encouraging a less traditional division of labour between the sexes. Yet 'We can measure the success of the hours strategy by the *change* it allows at home' (Phillips 1983:57) My empirical study was undertaken to see how likely men were to take on housework when they had more time at their disposal.

I based my hypothesis on a 'changing roles' perspective (Pleck 1979), which looks at concrete strategies that might bring about changes in gender roles within the family.[2] In order to identify possible mechanisms for change, it is therefore important to take a sample where a gender shift in the domestic burden is likely. I chose a sample of families where the wife was in full-time or at least part-time employment, whilst the husband was not employed, and where there were also children. My hypothesis was that under such family circumstances, the time available to undertake domestic tasks would be doubly altered. Men, not being in paid employment, would have more time to undertake domestic work; whilst women, being in the labour market, would have less. If there were also children in the family, the burden of domestic work would be relatively large, making changes both more imperative and more observable.

The sample families were obtained from a project examining employment potential in Sunderland, which involved a questionnaire interview with a 10 per cent sample of households in selected areas of the borough.[3] This household survey provided names and addresses of suitable families. In the event, it was found difficult to identify a sufficient number of families with unemployed husbands, employed wives and with children under 16 years old from the survey. This was perhaps scarcely surprising given the disincentives of the benefits system for women to work in these circumstances. This meant that the sample was less homogeneous than was originally intended in two respects. First, families with adult children still living at home were included, and second, families with non-employed men below the retirement age of 65. In particular, this latter meant the inclusion of men who were sick, either on a temporary or permanent basis. Just as Martin and Roberts (1984) have shown the flexibility and lack of clear-cut distinctions in any meaningful definition of women's unemployment, so, as job opportunities decline and long-term unemployment grows, the definition of unemployment for men also becomes less clear. In particular of course, men who have retired early or who are sick, but not incapable of work, may become 'discouraged workers' and give up seeking work given the poor prospects. When the characteristics of the sample families are examined in the next section, the difficulties of distinguishing between the categories of sick and unemployed are highlighted, which does much to reduce this sampling problem.

A homogenous sample is especially important for the research method adopted: that of a taped semi-structured interview. This method was adopted for two main reasons; the need for sensitivity in establishing the gender division of family work, and the difficulty of assessing how far change had taken place when husbands become unemployed. The method of using structured interviews is based on the theoretical framework of symbolic interactionism, whose key theoretical issue is the connection between social dynamics and historical change. It is true that survey techniques serve a useful purpose, and 'if by "social relations" we understand "relations between variables", we shall select the survey technique' (Bertaux 1981:35). But to understand the pattern of socio-structural relations, a 'life story' is more appropriate. Given the concern to identify mechanisms for change and constraints on change in household gender relations, the expression of what people already know about social life in this regard is best elicited from a semi-structured interview. Depth of understanding thus replaces breadth of knowledge by interviewing families whose experience is as homogeneous as possible with respect to gender patterns of employment, unemployment, and to children. In-depth taped interviews, then, allow for interviewees to provide meanings, understandings, and interpretations of the situation they are in.

The interview[4] lasted about an hour, and was intended to allow couples to tell a story about themselves. Early factual parts of the interview dealing with background and who does what in the household aimed to put people at their ease with fairly quick questions. A form on who undertook housework and childcare tasks was then filled in by the interviewer with the tape recorder switched on for the additional comments often made whilst husbands and wives were answering. The third part of the interview, designed to elicit gender variations in who did household or childcare tasks with the occurrence of unemployment, started with a brief employment history for wives and husbands. This was to help couples to cast their minds back to their earlier situation and make changes easier to recall. It was not until the end of the interview that people were asked about attitudes.

Interviews took place in the winter of 1985–6, and couples were interviewed together wherever possible. It was seen as important to get a joint view, for example, of who does what in the way of household tasks. A joint interview also provided an opportunity for any conflict of views to be made explicit. It became apparent on the few occasions when interviews had to be held separately that this could arouse suspicions and fears on the part of spouses about what the other partner might say. There was also a pragmatic reason for holding a joint interview: the limited time available on a six month project. The two interviewers[5] were of course aware of the need to afford spouses an equal hearing in the context of a joint interview, and this was encouraged by asking wives and husbands a similar set of questions addressed to each in turn.

Whilst the response rate for the pilot stage was not encouraging, that for the main sample was a very respectable 82 per cent, and particularly encouraging for an in-depth interview lasting an hour. Of the thirty interviews held, husband and wife were interviewed separately, in two, one interview was with the husband only and two were with the wife only. One of the latter was a lengthy doorstep interview, so that there were only twenty-nine forms on the performance of household tasks. The doorstep interview with Mrs Ward[6] provided considerable insights into why people refused to give interviews, and it is worth pausing to hear what she had to say.

The two major reasons why Mrs Ward did not want to take part were time constraints, and that it was too depressing. With regard to the former, she said that she works every morning, and visits the hospital in the afternoons and evenings, whilst her husband, who is an electrician, is out a lot mending relatives' appliances. The family situation is also very depressing. Her husband has not had a job for nearly a year, and has only had a few short-term jobs – one lasting 10 months and others for 6 weeks – since he took redundancy 4 years ago. The short-term jobs cause problems in sorting benefits out. She herself has been working mornings as a home help for twelve years. The old people rely on her, and she even visits them on Saturday, which is officially her day off.

But I get really depressed. To be honest, I was rock bottom yesterday. I came home and cried and I didn't want anyone to see me in such a state. I keep my job on hoping he'll get a job. But I'm only working for £4,[7] and then, the old people, they rely on me. I've never been so close to packing it in. It can't be good for my husband, seeing me getting up in the morning to earn nothing. It probably wouldn't be so bad if I was at home.

What he wants is a job. I mean there's twenty years of work in him [Mr Ward is 46]. He's lost his status. It's no good me working full-time and him becoming the housewife. Switching roles isn't what he wants, work is what he knows. It isn't as if he hasn't tried for jobs. Even if he gets one, they'd pay such low wages now, I'd have to carry on with mine.

I think if we talked to you it would come over that we were bitter and angry, when most of the time we get by. I mean I have my very low days; then I might be alright again for a few months. It's very stressful at times.

This summing-up of why Mrs Ward would not take part speaks for itself, yet it also gives a flavour that comes through in parts of many of the interviews. The bravery in the face of adversity of many of the men and women who spoke to us was impressive. It was people's willingness to speak under these sorts of circumstances that was striking, rather than their unwillingness.[8]

The characteristics of the Wearside families

What were the families who were interviewed like? Several features are of particular interest to the research design: family structure, and in particular the size of families; the employment pattern of wives; and the context of non-employment for husbands. Some interesting factors also emerge from a consideration of the characteristics of the thirty families. First, the employment experience of wives and husbands indicates an overwhelmingly working-class sample. Second, many of their characteristics would seem to reinforce the likelihood of a traditional gender division of labour. Third, although some of the husbands were not unemployed according to official definitions, the interview material revealed that nearly three-quarters of them could appropriately be classified as unemployed. The final feature indicates that the sample families were historically representative of working males in Sunderland. The previous employment pattern of husbands, though rather different from that of the 1980s, corresponded well with the structure of employment in the borough up to 1970.

Let us look first of all at family structure. The couples in the sample were predominantly middle-aged. There were no young spouses for only one wife was under 30, with nearly three-quarters of husbands aged between 35 and 49, and half the wives aged between 35 and 44. Family size was noticeably large: in terms of total family size – including children who had left home – nearly three-quarters of the families had four or more children while there was one family with eight children, and just one with an only child. Of more relevance to the burden of housework and childcare was the number of children living at home, where half the families had two children, and the average number of children at home per family in the sample was 2.3. Also of considerable relevance to the level of household work was the age of those children at home. Approximately half of the families had youngest children of school age and under, with the other half having only adult children. In all, seventy children were living in the thirty families, and again about half these children were adult (over 16 years old) while twenty-one were of secondary school age and eleven of primary school age. There was only one pre-school child in the sample. It has already been pointed out that the original research design was to use only families with children of under 16 years old. It made it more difficult to generalise about childcare tasks with a less homogeneous sample. Nevertheless there were still a respectable number of families where the youngest child was of primary and of secondary school age (six and seven families respectively).

Turning now to the employment pattern of wives, there was, first, a substantial commitment to the labour market in terms of hours worked. Five worked full-time, and wives working over 30 hours – treated as full-time in terms of legislation – made up very nearly a quarter of the sample. Indeed over half were out at work for over 20 hours. Second, and contrary to stereotypes, the length of time that women had been in their present employment indicated considerable stability of employment and distinctly low rates of turnover. Thus only two wives had been less than a year in their job, and whilst two had had their jobs for over 15 years, eleven had held them between 10 and 15 years. The type of job held was nevertheless overwhelmingly in traditional female areas. Thus eight women were cleaners of various sorts, but including one supervisor, and there were four shop assistants, and five home helps. Amongst the most responsible jobs were a nursery nurse, and a warden of sheltered accommodation for the elderly. The most non-traditional in employment terms were the operator and the self-employed person, although her occupation was a traditional one, a hairdresser.

Third, women's pay was almost universally characterised by its low level. Whatever definition of low pay we take, only two women could be regarded as escaping low pay; both worked in the manufacturing sector, as an operator and a cleaning supervisor. The average take-home pay in the sample was £1.90 an hour at 1985–6 prices, well below low pay definitions.[9] Whilst it comes as no surprise that women in such traditionally female occupations should be low paid, it is worth remembering that the seven women who worked over 30 hours were effectively family breadwinners. Indeed all the women except two had husbands who received at most only a state benefit. Additionally, nearly a quarter of the women in the sample – all of whose husbands are on supplementary benefit – were in effect earning £4 a week, due to the pound for pound deductions made from their husband's benefit if they earned more than that amount. This provides further evidence of the attachment of these women to the labour market.

What of the nature of non-employment for the husbands in the sample? As we have already seen, husbands were not all straightforwardly unemployed. Official government measures of unemployment would make under half the sample unemployed, and include only the eight men on unemployment benefit and six on supplementary benefit. Three more men received no state benefit because their wives were earning just over supplementary benefit level wages: they would have appeared under previous official methods. It is worth noting that five of the eleven men on invalidity benefit had received redundancy pay when they left work, indicating that they were originally made unemployed. In a tight labour market there is of course a considerable incentive to take redundancy if one is also not well, since invalidity benefit provides a noticeably better standard of living than do other forms of state benefit. It was not surprising that people were prepared to take redundancy and leave the job market with high unemployment rates and the generally low level of wages which men received in their last job.

Low levels of official unemployment in the sample contrasted sharply with the fuller picture of the labour market position gleaned from the in-depth interview in which qualitative judgements could be made about the nature of non-employment. Here it became apparent that poor job prospects combined with the existence of long-term unemployment required more flexible definitions of unemployment for men. It was also clear that sickness could on the one hand limit job search, whilst on the other, that the existence of sickness might be a function of either unemployment or of work itself, in the case of accident or stress. When all those men who were seeking work, or intended to do so within a short space of time – for example after a short illness – were included within the unemployed, twenty-two, or nearly three-quarters could be classified as unemployed.

The remaining eight men were permanently sick, and on invalidity benefit, and were not seeking work. It was certainly problematic that the sample was extended to include these non-employed husbands. The extension can however be justified on a number of grounds. First, half of these permanently sick men had received redundancy pay when they first left work, and it is usual to consider individuals made redundant as unemployed. Second, in terms of the organisation of domestic tasks, it was found that families with permanently sick husbands and with unemployed husbands behaved approximately the same. Additionally, in three cases, permanent sickness was work-related, with two industrial accidents and one case of stress. Fourth, it could be argued that, in a labour market with more employment opportunities, most of these men might find jobs compatible with their health disability. Finally of course, there is movement over time between the categories of permanently sick and unemployed, and this had happened to several of the men in the sample. It was thus reasonable, although not ideal, for the sample to include men who were permanently sick.

Turning now to the length of time for which husbands had not been working, ten had been out of work for less than a year, though none had been out of work for less than 5 months. It was felt important that husbands should have been out of work for a minimum of 3 months to allow time for the effects of unemployment to express themselves. Excluding the permanently sick, this meant that the rate of long term unemployment of those unemployed for a year or over in the sample was 55 per cent, which was very close to the rate for Sunderland borough of 56 per cent (Stone and Stevens 1985:30). Length of non-work can be contrasted with the length of time that husbands spent in the job they held immediately prior to their period of non-employment. Over a quarter of the sample had been in their jobs for more than 20 years, while nineteen men (over 60 per cent) had been in their jobs for over 5 years. Like their wives, this indicates considerable stability of employment: these are almost entirely men with a tradition of regular work. It also gives an indication of the change in terms of loss of stability that unemployment or ill health must bring.

In terms of previous employment of husbands, the employment structure of the sample is somewhat different from that for Wearside in 1981 (see Stone and Stevens 1985:chapter 3). Ten per cent of the sample were employed in what is now British Coal, and this is an under-representation compared with the 1981 figure of 16.5 per cent of male employment in the primary sector in 1981. On the other hand, 56 per cent of the sample men were employed in manufacturing (including shipbuilding), whilst in 1981 only 36 per cent of Wearside men were employed in this sector. This was compensated for by an under-representation of services in the sample (30 per cent) as against 38 per cent of men on Wearside generally being employed in services. The employment structure of the sample was in fact noticeably skewed towards manufacturing in general and towards shipbuilding in particular. Indeed it could be argued that the sample was more representative of the 'aristocracy of labour' which characterised Sunderland prior to 1970. It has however already been remarked that the figures for take-home pay which men received in their last job gave the impression of generally low rates of pay.

It will be noticed then, that although the sample was deliberately chosen to highlight possible changes in the gender division of household work, in that wives were working whilst their husbands were not in paid work, many of the characteristics of the sample families would popularly and intuitively be seen as tending to reinforce the traditional gender division of domestic labour. For example, whilst there are unfortunately no historical studies, the North East is a region where the gender division of labour has traditionally been seen as strong.[10] The fact that the sample is both working-class and predominantly middle aged provides further reinforcement. The employment characteristics of men and women only underline this further: it has been shown that the husbands tend to come from the skilled 'aristocracy of labour' whilst their wives command universally low wages. Such features reinforce ideas of the male breadwinner, the opposite side of the coin to stereotypes of housewife and mother. The latter is further underlined by the large families found in the sample. The characteristics of the sample therefore make the results of the empirical work particularly striking.

Having provided a background for the empirical work, future Setting the scenes will tell the story for individual families of specific aspects of the interviews, so that for example, Chapter 2 on structural economic change is preceded by a description of the changing employment experiences of four of the Wearside couples. Wives and husbands will speak for themselves of their experiences.

Let us now start to establish a conceptual framework for examining the links between economic restructuring and the internal dynamics of the household by specifying the place of the household sector within the wider formal economy.

Chapter 1

Introduction: the household sector in total economic activity

The role of the household in the economy

What are the effects of economic change on the unpaid work done largely within households? More specifically, how can household work strategies be linked to national structural change, itself related to changes in the world economy? This book is concerned to answer this question by drawing on and developing the work currently being done in this sphere, with particular reference to its implications for changing roles for both men and women. Ideology on the one hand, and the role of the state in providing benefits on the other, have important parts to play in influencing such role changes. Whilst there is now far more awareness of both the need to account for work done by women as well as men, and to theorise on the relationship between men's and women's work; the significance of the unpaid, unmeasured, sector of the economy – much of whose work is undertaken within the household – still remains largely unexplored.

This book is about those economic processes which are not encompassed by money or commodity relations, and the extent to which economic restructuring in the formal economy brings about changes in such economic processes, together with their social effects. Since activities and transactions not subject to the pricing mechanism have regularly been excluded from the concerns of economists, the effects of de-industrialisation and the decline of full employment under advanced capitalism on such economic processes have not been fully explored. It has become accepted that we cannot trivialise the personal by seeing it simply as personal. The family is at the heart of personal experiences; yet the family is one of a range of informal institutions which rarely feature in economic accounts or theorising. As this book will be arguing, the family in particular, and the economically unmeasured sector in general, are not an alternative society. They are a set of activities which are complementary to the formal, money economy, but with a personal life style. Indeed, to put it in a Marxist theoretical framework, 'an analysis of the relationship between the family and the labour process must be central to any account of the mode of production as a whole' (Redclift 1985:94).

The household has been seen as one of two basic units of analysis in economics for more than a century. The firm is the other. Yet the focus of attention has been on the individual male earner, thanks to the emphasis on employment of a male breadwinner as the only significant form of work. It is important not to exaggerate the importance of the stereotypical family unit, made up of a male breadwinner, his non-working wife and their 2.4 children, for such families make up only 15 per cent of all households. It is nevertheless surprising how consistently economists have regarded those entering the labour market as individuals rather than as members of a household unit; whilst at the same time regarding the household as an undifferentiated individual and not as a group.

The household has been regarded as a 'black box' by economists, making it unnecessary to examine the gender pattern of either consumption, or of expenditure within this basic unit. Similarly, the significance of the household in terms of production was largely ignored, as for example its role in the rearing of a future labour force. 'Economists hardly recognise that [the household] exists, caring little beyond that it consumes an adequate number of dishwashers and continues to save at an appropriate rate' (Burns 1977:3). As a response to the Women's Movement, academic sociologists in particular, took the initiative in raising questions about what constituted 'work', looking at work more widely and making connections between paid and unpaid work. Gender was also introduced as a significant factor, both in the labour market itself and within the household. The issue of women as dual workers both in the home and in the job market became incorporated into academic thinking.

In addition, the structure of employment in the developed industrialised economies has been changing, with a shift from manufacturing to service employment. This restructuring process has had both a marked regional or spatial dimension to it, as well as a strong gender component. At the same time, levels of unemployment have risen, and its structure has altered. Whilst levels are currently falling, the forces of technological change and those of international competition are such that unemployment is likely to remain high by post-war standards, at least in the regions. In addition, it has become apparent that the changing structure of employment is not just a function of recession, but of expansion too, something which has been explained in terms of the increasing use of 'flexibility' amongst the workforce and in firms. In Britain it is particularly male manual workers who have been subject to unemployment, whilst job opportunities for women – albeit often part-time – have remained relatively buoyant.

To what extent do changing patterns of male unemployment affect the gender characteristics of work within the household? Popularly, there are some perceptions that these economic changes have led to the fading of the 'old patriarchal order' within the household, expressed, for example, in Shirley Conran's (1975) ideas of the 'career woman', or more academically, with Young and Wilmott's *Symmetrical Family* (1973). It is noticeable that such views of progressive change in response to wider economic pressures relate mainly to middle-class and professional families. In order to analyse the effects of men no longer being in paid work on the gender basis of family work strategies, it is important first of all to be clear on what work strategies are available to families in developed market economies. This means that definitions of formal paid, as well as informal, unpaid work are essential, together with a clear specification of the relationship between the individual, the household, the community, and the economy more generally. It is important to develop a typology of total economic activity, and consider the relationship between the various elements involved.

The boundary between the formal economy and the household sector is established in how production decisions within the household are made. The crucial question becomes: 'On what basis do people choose to do some things themselves (household production), and to have others done by someone else (formal economy)?' (Smith 1986:162). This can alternatively be put in terms of the choice individuals and families make about how to earn their income, and whether they choose work for self-consumption or for income. Indeed, the relationship between waged and other work constitutes the reason for the connection between the reproductive cycle of the family unit and the general process of accumulation and development under capitalism (Mingione 1985). Not merely do these concerns throw light on the conventional constructs of employed, unemployed, and people not in the labour force as used in labour market analysis, they are also steeped in considerations where gender is of fundamental importance. It is not appropriate to explain the basis on which the complementary economy functions simply in terms of economic gain, and when we consider the full range of economic institutions, both informal and formal, it becomes imperative to look beyond the stereotype of 'rational economic man' (*sic*) to gain a proper understanding of people's motivation.

It is important to realise that the household is a productive economic institution, which, like the firm, produces goods and services with a tangible economic value and employs labour and capital. The difference is that 'The producer produces *for* the household; the consumer produces *within* the household' (Burns 1977:61). This contrast between producer and consumer indicates how the household is excluded from the ideology of the market, for the household acquires only such goods, and provides only such services as it deems necessary. What then of the relationship of the household to the formal economy? Economists' concern with the monetised, legitimate activities of the private and public sectors of market and state, means that activities and transactions not subject to the pricing mechanism tend to be ignored. This has of course been the factor at work behind failing to consider the economic role of women, but also, and importantly, it excludes the 'informal economy', within which the household falls. In order to specify the relationship between the household and the formal economy it is essential to have a more precise understanding of the nature of the non-formal economy. The latter is, unfortunately a very diverse sector, which has been seen to include not just housework, but also voluntary work, DIY, white-collar crime, and the 'black economy', to name but a few of the other elements that have been put under its rubric. The non-formal economy has a correspondingly confusing variety of names, both for the sector as a whole, and for its component parts. Let us therefore turn to developing a typology for the institutional structure of the economy as a whole, so that the household economy can be clearly located in relation to the rest of the economy.

An institutional model: the household in the complementary economy

Economics pays considerable attention to the institutional structures of the formal economy. Orthodox economics focuses on market structure, its effects on competition and on the prices charged by firms and their levels of output. The theory of the firm identifies three basic institutional structures. Monopoly firms are single producers of a product, and hence there is a danger of over-pricing. Oligopolies have a few producers in competition, so that there may be collusion over prices, or price leadership. Third there is imperfect competition, where advertising and 'product differentiation' become the form that competition takes. Within the Marxist paradigm, the emphasis is on the institutional form taken by accumulation. During the accumulation process, the form taken by 'many capitals' in competition changes. Under modern capitalism there is not merely competitive, or non-monopoly, capital; but also monopoly capital, financial capital, international capital, and state capital.

Both paradigms have similarly paid considerable attention to the institutions of the labour market. Again the orthodox focus is on the determination of prices, which in this case are wages. Marxists are concerned with the labour process and its role in accumulation. There has been little attention paid within either paradigm to the institutional structures relating to the reproduction of labour power or those which lie

17

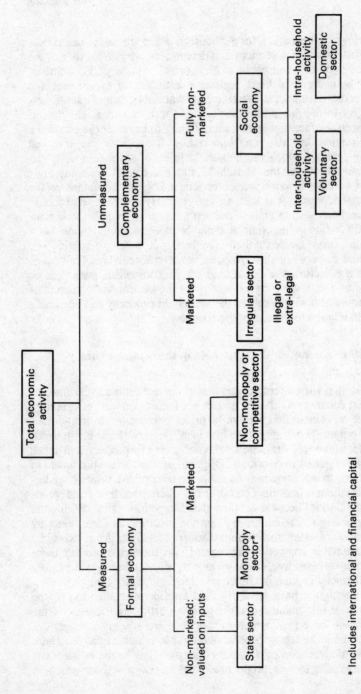

Figure 1.1 A typology of productive economic institutions

* Includes international and financial capital

on the margins between this and the accumulation of capital. It is precisely this gap in the attention to institutional structures that the typology in Figure 1.1 attempts to address.

The typology is drawn up with the requirements of this study in mind: namely to specify the effects of structural changes in employment in the formal sector on household work strategies, which fall partly in the formal and partly in the non-formal economy. To take account of total economic activity within a developed economy, the formal sector of that economy can be contrasted with the complementary economy, which in turn can be subdivided into two sectors: the irregular economy and the social economy. The social economy itself consists of two subsectors many of whose tasks may be undertaken in either the household sector or in the voluntary sector.

Broadly speaking, the division between the formal and the complementary economy follows the line between measured and unmeasured economic activity. Formal economic activity is recorded in the national income accounts (Smith 1986). But just as the formal economy has two sectors: one private and marketed, the other a non-marketed state sector; so too does the complementary economy. These are the marketed irregular sector and the non-marketed social economy. The output of the social economy is not sold on the market, and its labour is unpaid. The institutions of the social economy are self-generated informal ones, which operate independently of regular economic institutions, and can be characterised as personalised institutional forms. There are essentially two sorts of institutional relations in the social economy: intra-household relations and inter-household ones.

Within the household sector, work for self-consumption for the family unit takes place. As Mingione (1985) and others have suggested, household work can be broken down into domestic work, consisting of housework and caring, especially for children, but also for the sick, elderly, and handicapped; and extra self-consumption. Extra self-consumption can be distinguished by the fact that although these goods and services could be purchased on the market, the work is actually done within the household on an unpaid basis. Examples of extra self-consumption tend to be quite limited in developed economies, consisting largely of DIY and home improvements, making clothes or knitting, and some forms of food processing such as brewing and bread or jam making. In developing countries, extra self-consumption is a more extensive category and can include water fetching, fire wood collection, wild food gathering and food processing activities such as grain milling, as well as housebuilding. It is perhaps worth realising however, that even in the world's wealthiest nation, the United States, 20 per cent of all single family dwellings are self-built, and that there are high rates of self-building in Germany and Canada too.

In the voluntary sector, work is also unpaid, but this time it is undertaken between households. It can consist of what Bulmer (1986) aptly calls 'neighbouring', or of self-help or voluntary work. Extra self-consumption may also be transferred from the individual household and undertaken on an inter-household basis. In addition, the childcare and other caring functions of domestic work may be partly transferred to the voluntary sector on an unpaid basis. As Stuart Henry sees it, this sector 'is the embodiment of the counter culture. . . . More generally it is the way in which people come together to satisfy needs that have not been met by the formal system of the regular economy' (Henry 1981:19).

Whilst it may not always be easy to draw the boundaries between the voluntary and the irregular sectors, a feature of the latter is that its output is marketed. What distinguishes it from the formal economy is its institutional framework as either illegal or extra-legal. The irregular sector thus contains a huge range of economic activities, from corporate crime, white-collar crime, and tax evasion to pilfering, fiddling, and working and claiming. The boundaries of the irregular economy are flexible over time, because they are defined by changing social attitudes as codified in changes in the law. Historically, for example, what had been wood-gathering, grazing, and game rights, became wood theft, trespassing, and poaching respectively (Henry 1981:14). Within the irregular economy a distinction can be made between illegal and extra-legal activities, where the latter avoid paying taxes or establish false entitlements to state support.

I have contrasted the formal economy with the complementary economy because the latter plays precisely that role: it complements the formal economy. The complementary sector is neither parasitic nor residual, and it operates in the interstices of formal institutions, not as an alternative society but as a complementary economic activity to the formal. So, for example, while the state and the private sector within the formal economy may have taken on some aspects of the production and reproduction of labour power (such as education, training, pension provision, and health), the household sector still retains much of its responsibility here.

Similarly the irregular sector can be seen as a mirror of the free market capitalist spirit, indeed a caricature of it. In a rare study of corporate crime, Clinard and Yeager assert that 'Corporate crime is indicative of the distribution of power in our society' (Clinard and Yeager 1980:21), and that it provides an indication of society's degree of hypocrisy by countenancing upper-class deception and calling it 'shrewd business practice' . What is more,

> the desire to increase or maintain current profits is the critical
> factor in a wide range of corporate deviance, from refusal to install

pollution control equipment to well planned decisions to make a shoddy product that will wear out and need replacing.

(Clinard and Yeager 1980:47)

On the other hand, the irregular sector can also be seen as complementing the role of the state as a redistributor of income; this is the case when the irregular economy provides an alternative or additional source of employment for people, and acts as a form of income support.

A further contrast between the formal and the complementary economy can be made by considering the contradiction between the public, and the private or personal, in each sector. In the formal economy, as was first pointed out by Lenin (1916) and other Marxist theorists of the monopoly stage of capitalism, the concentration and centralisation of capital into large units facilitates the interiorisation of the contradiction between social and private within the internal calculation of the single, large-scale economic unit (Wheelock 1984). Market relations no longer hold between subsidiaries of multinational companies, who use administrative prices instead, and one third of international trade is made up of such transactions. Indeed money is no longer even used in the barter-based counter-trading deals which make up a further third of world trade.

The family and the household sector are at the opposite end of this contradiction between the social and the private, and also interiorise the contradiction. On the one hand it can seem, for example, that families choose between self-consumption alternatives, or whether to have children and how many they will have. Pahl and Wallace can point to a process of domestication as the 'product of a value system which puts home-centred activities as the central focus of a distinctive life style' Pahl and Wallace (1985:219). On the other hand this personalised organisational form can be constrained by the market, or by public political decisions taken by the state to change the pattern of distribution. The household economy becomes a strategy for economic survival (Bradley 1986), and informal institutions can act as a mask for the failures of the official economy and an excuse for governments to offload responsibilities. The social economy then provides goods or services which are either hard to obtain, or too expensive, given the price mechanism or levels of taxation. An example of the former type of provision is self-help; of the latter, home improvements.

Indeed the same types of activity are to be found in the formal and in the irregular sectors; what is different is the nature of these activities. In the irregular economy, the size and scale of activity is generally smaller, with direct distribution and little specialisation of labour. Levels of investment are low, and activity is often intermittent. Levels of return for work vary more widely, and pricing is idiosyncratic, in part because the relations between providers and users are often grounded in personal ties. In addition, however, it is not easy to distinguish the irregular from the social economy for 'Many exchanges that are irregular involve an unrecorded exchange of money and are virtually indistinguishable from similar transactions that do not involve overt payment' (Ferman and Berndt 1981:30).

The complementary economy therefore has an intermediate status in the social reproduction processes of capitalism: on the one hand it performs a major role in producing and reproducing labour power, on the other hand it can reproduce – in the irregular sector – non-monopoly capital, or even monopoly capital, in the case of corporate crime. So, for example, formal work reflects the fundamental cost of labour in the reproduction process, together with monetary consumption capacity, and it contributes to the state fiscal system. When individuals combine work in the formal and the irregular economy, this is a source of income, but it does not reflect the full costs of labour, and it cheats the fiscal system in part. Work undertaken entirely in the irregular sector is not detected and so cheats the fiscal system.

The balance between work for self-consumption and for income (whether formal or informal) is determined by the qualitative and quantitative structure of labour demand, including its gender structure and the role of state intervention. A classification system for the economy as a whole provides a framework for analysing the relationship between changes in the structure of the formal and complementary economies, together with the process of accumulation and economic growth. This raises a number of important issues which go beyond that of classification, to the practical and theoretical implications of the typology. A theory of capitalist regulation involves the articulation of the laws of capital accumulation and of the laws of competition. The laws of capital accumulation involve the study of the transformation of wage relations, while those of competition mean clarifying the transformation of inter-capitalist relations. Neither set of laws can be examined within the formal economy alone, but require a study of the articulation between the formal and the complementary sectors of the economy. Finally, there is also the issue of motivation: how far do motivations in the complementary economy differ from those in the formal economy, or are the same kinds of rules at work? These issues are taken up again in the Conclusions, in the light of the analysis of the empirical study in Part II of the book, but let me continue my introductory task by looking at the size of the complementary economy, and of the household sector within that.

Measuring the work of the complementary economy

To what extent does the size of the complementary economy in general and of the domestic economy in particular justify the attention that will be paid to it in this study? Since the sector is largely unmeasured in official statistics, a first task should be to assess the validity of the methods that have been used to measure it, and we shall find very large discrepancies in the orders of magnitude suggested by different studies. In general, most attention has been paid to attempting to measure some of the constituent parts of the complementary economy, particularly the domestic sector, and some parts of the irregular sector. Only limited work has been done on the voluntary sector, or on measuring corporate crime as an element of the irregular sector. There have, however, been two studies which provide some indication of the overall size of the complementary economy, through surveys of households' use of it, both of which have undertaken an in-depth study of a relatively small scale area, one in the United States, and one on the Isle of Sheppey.

In Detroit, Ferman and Berndt (1981) found that 60 per cent of the services households used were secured through the social economy, within the household or from friends or relatives without pay; a further 10 per cent derived from the irregular sector with monetary payment; whilst only the remaining 30 per cent was purchased from the formal economy. Such figures provide striking evidence for the importance of the complementary economy, but it must be remembered that Ferman and Berndt were looking only at a selection of services, not at the purchase of goods, and it is generally perceived that services are particularly predominant in both the domestic and the irregular sectors.

In his British study, Pahl (1984) also took a selection of groups of tasks (home maintenance, house improvement and renovation, routine housework, domestic production, car maintenance, and childcare) amounting to forty one tasks in all. Pahl looked at how far these tasks were done inside the household in the domestic sector; or in the voluntary, irregular, or the formal sectors. Perhaps wisely, Pahl does not speculate on the proportion of work undertaken in each economy in households as a whole, though he does comment that 'a remarkable amount of work is done by members of individual households for themselves' (Pahl 1984:232). He is actually more interested in making links between patterns of types of work and household structure, particularly in terms of number of earners and the stage of the domestic life cycle. In addition, in order to discover which households will use what types of labour in which sector, he develops a series of indices which cover not simply the number of tasks, but the range of tasks. Thus the self-provisioning index 'measures the spread of activity that given households do using the labour of members of the households themselves' (Pahl 1984:233), whilst the formal provision of services scale does the same for the formal economy. The informal labour scale includes tasks done by labour outside the household, but which may be paid or unpaid. Although the informal labour scale includes elements of both the voluntary and the irregular sectors, Pahl remarks on how very modestly households score on this last scale, and concludes: 'This is an emphatic refutation of the notion that the use of informal labour is very widespread' (ibid.:241).

Let us turn to the efforts to measure the social economy, which concentrate on the domestic as a subsector. Goldschmidt-Clermont (1987) suggests three common characteristics of this economy: that the household's dwelling is the main *locus* of production and consumption, that labour is supplied by unpaid household members, and that the goods and services produced are directly consumed by the household without monetary transaction. Important from the point of view of measurement is that these characteristics make domestic activities fully non-market, in the sense that both inputs and outputs are non-marketed. This is unlike government services in the formal economy for example, where inputs can be valued on a market basis. A further major problem for measurement is that domestic activities are only partly undertaken to satisfy economic needs; the rest comply with personal needs and social roles. So, for example, Robinson *et al.* (1972) find that sleeping, eating, and personal hygiene take up $10\frac{1}{2}$ hours a day or 44 per cent of a 24 hour day, and that free time is $4\frac{1}{3}$ hours on average for the twelve countries studied. Should the definition of domestic production include activities necessary to the reproduction of labour power such as sleeping and leisure? The 'third person criterion' has actually been used to distinguish economic activity (considered as production) from the rest, by asking the question whether the performance of an activity can be delegated to a paid outsider or not. The example of surrogate motherhood indicates that the third person criterion is by no means a hard and fast one however.

There are three methods of measuring the domestic economy, which depend on the units used – physical or monetary values – and whether done via inputs or outputs (Goldschmidt-Clermont 1987). First, there are input related evaluations of household production based on the volume of inputs, which can be measured either in terms of the number of workers involved or in terms of time taken, the majority of studies taking the latter course. The problems of this method include those of recall versus observation as a method of study, the issue of simultaneous activities, and that time inputs do not reflect work intensity. None of the studies looked at by Goldschmidt-Clermont sets time inputs into domestic activities at less than 25 per cent of total labour inputs. *The*

Economist (1987) gives unsourced figures for the average British adult spending 21 hours a week in paid employment and 23 hours in productive activities in the home, while Robinson *et al.* (1972:118) indicate that the time devoted to paid work is very nearly doubled when domestic work is added to formal work. Such figures suggest that GNP falls short of output by between 25 and 50 per cent of the population's productive activity when the domestic economy is taken into account. There is therefore a major gender bias in officially measured work, for, the world over, domestic economic activity is mainly performed by women.

The second method is again input-related, but based on the value of inputs. The crucial question here relates to how to measure this value. Wage-based evaluations may measure the wages of substitute household workers, domestic servants, or nannies, by comparison with wages paid in similar market enterprises; the cost of upkeep of children or adults in institutional homes; or the 'wage foregone' or opportunity cost of time. All wage-based evaluations need first to determine the volume of labour inputs, and this in itself is problematic; the values selected for imputation then act as coefficients. Particularly heavy criticisms have been levied against the opportunity cost of time method based on the 'new home economics' school of Gary Becker (1965). Can one substitute market and non-market work? We have already seen that Pahl suggests not. Even in developed countries, where in theory the market provides many human needs, some non-market time is necessary for survival. In practice 'non-market time appears largely as complementary to market time and is governed by other criteria than market time' (Goldschmidt-Clermont (1987:34). Whilst use of the wages of substitute workers is more valid, it is still a mistake to equate the value of labour input with gross output value since 'household workers' wages are determined by labour market factors which bear no relation to the value of household output' (ibid.:32). Smith (1986) points to a thorough survey of American studies of the size of the domestic economy which suggests that it might be equivalent to 30 to 40 per cent of GDP, while *The Economist* (1987) quotes a German study which places it as high as 70 per cent of GDP.

The final method need not detain us long, for it has not been used at all extensively despite the advantages that Goldschmidt-Clermont sees in it. It is an output-related evaluation of household production, which measures the volume of output, where either producer prices or retail prices can be used for imputation. The advantages of the method are that it is based on the same principles as national accounts, that it accounts for production circumstances, and that it avoids the problems of work intensity and of simultaneous activities as well as cultural and social bias.

The significance of the domestic sector in the economy as a whole is also highlighted by the importance of household investment as a proportion of total investment. In his American study, Burns (1977) argues that home ownership gives an imputed cash income larger than the dividends paid out to all corporations in the United States. Whilst in 1900, single family residential construction was only one fifth of business construction, by 1960 it had exceeded business construction. Cars are the second largest investment by households. Indeed, annual investment in major consumer durables now exceeds producer investment. Burns' theme that this signifies the rise of household capitalism has been taken up by Gershuny (1978) for the British economy in terms of a self-service economy.

Whilst estimates of the size of the domestic economy may seem to vary widely, those for the irregular economy are more broadly spread still. This is scarcely surprising given the very varied nature of the activities within this sector, and the fact that its illegal or extra-legal nature will inevitably mean that those involved will be chary of providing information. There are five major sorts of irregular economic activity: tax evasion, pilfering and fiddling, working and claiming, corporate crime, and criminal activities including drug dealing and prostitution. There have, as far as I know, been no attempts to quantify the last two categories within the British economy. Some guestimates have been made for the extent of pilfering and fiddling, and there have been a few studies of the extent of second job holding.

The major efforts at measuring the irregular economy have been devoted to overall estimates of the extent of tax evasion and working and claiming. In his careful overall assessment of the literature on the size of this element of the irregular economy, Smith is very much inclined to caution, and whilst he feels that it is unlikely to be less than about 3 per cent of GDP, 'there is no convincing evidence that the black economy in the UK approaches anything like 15 per cent of GDP. Even 5 per cent would seem a high, though not inconceivable, upper bound (Smith 1986:191). This is very small compared with the orders of magnitude suggested for the domestic economy.

What though of the other elements of the irregular economy? The only comprehensive account of corporate crime was undertaken in the United States, and in it Clinard and Yeager make no attempt to measure its size, though they provide some figures on orders of magnitude in particular categories which suggest that corporate crime overall may be of far greater importance than those elements of the irregular economy where attention has been directed to date. The costs of corporate crime

involve not only large financial losses but also injuries, deaths and health hazards. They also involve the incalculable costs of the damage done to the physical environment and the great social costs of the erosion of the moral base of society.

(Clinard and Yeager 1980:8).

The authors contrast the illegal overcharging to the tune of $1 billion by nine major oil companies in 1979, with the largest robbery in the United States to date of $4 million. Lipert (in Ekins 1986) suggests that the costs of corporate violence, in terms of death and injury through pollution and occupational hazards, should be deducted from GNP, to allow for the damage done to the quality of life. The irregular sector must thus be far larger than 5 per cent of GNP when corporate crime is included. It is, however, difficult to hazard a guess as to how much larger it should be. The concept of 'adjusted' national product put forward by Lipert does nevertheless suggest that it would be substantial.

It is still the case that overall, such estimates as we have indicate that the size of the social economy dwarfs that of the irregular sector. This would be so, even were only the domestic sector considered, since this alone makes up some 40 per cent of GNP. It is nevertheless unfortunate that the only indications for the size of the voluntary sector derive from survey information, where for example Hatch (1981) shows that 10 per cent of adults take part in voluntary work at least once a month. It is interesting that analysts of social policy reach the general conclusion that such work is performed predominantly by middle aged, middle class women. What is apparent is that the complementary economy *in toto* involves orders of magnitude that are at least comparable with those of the formal economy, and as such justifies far more attention than has been paid to it to date. This book concerns itself overwhelmingly with analysis of the social economy, concentrating within that on the domestic sector, for analysis of the irregular sector would require extensive study using a very different methodology.

Setting the scene 2

Changing employment experiences

Mr and Mrs Bolam: electrician and cleaning supervisor

When Mr and Mrs Bolam were both in work they were amongst the best paid couples in the sample. Mr Bolam was an electrician for over 20 years with what became Cape Insulation, whilst his wife had been a cleaning supervisor in a local manufacturing branch plant for 8 years. Cape Insulation (a subsidiary of Charter Consolidated) took over the Washington factory of Newalls Insulation Ltd in 1980, wishing to acquire extra capacity in what was thought to be an expanding market for glass fibre insulation, and making Cape the second largest producer. However, in the event the market declined, and Cape sold two of its plants to Pilkington Bros, and closed its Washington factory just as its investment programme was completed, in what may well have been part of a financial deal struck between the two companies (Stone and Stevens 1985). Mr Bolam was thus made redundant in December 1984, and at the time of the interview, had been on unemployment benefit for 11 months.

As an electrician Mr Bolam was responsible for maintaining equipment and repairing it as the need arose, and he liked the variety in his job. He worked long hours ('as many as God sent'), getting paid overtime of course, but 'it was a case of once I was there, I was available for work to do whatever happened'. As his wife put it, 'it was a case of work and bed', but she appreciated the fact that his job let him use 'his brain as well as his hands'. Mr. Bolam had been an active trade unionist and a shop steward, and expressed himself as a strong opponent of low wages, and a supporter of a national minimum wage. Since his redundancy he has made 'umpteen' applications for jobs, but at 46, 'I canna get a job now. I'm too old. According to them [the Job Centre] anyway.'

Mrs Bolam went back to work shortly after their second daughter (now 13) was born, getting her cleaning job through her sister-in-law. Four years later, not long after her youngest daughter was born, her sister-in-law died, and as the most experienced of the cleaners, she was given her supervisor's position. She now works a fixed 3½ hours a day, starting at 3.30 p.m. and is responsible for fourteen staff. A while back however, she used to work 'all the time. If anything went wrong there, why the phone would ring and I'd have to go down'. She now deals with all the little messages when she arrives at work: 'it works smashing. And I've got more time in the house'.

Mrs Bolam said that whilst she used to work for her benefit, she now works for 'ours; a woman stands a better chance of a job than a man'. There are two daughters living at home, whilst their oldest – aged 18 – lives with her grandmother to keep her company. Since the eldest has only a part-time job as a shop-assistant, she sometimes needs help with buying 'big things'. Her mother points out how modest the demands of their eldest daughter are: 'she goes out once a week, that lassie'.

Mr and Mrs O'Brien: moulder and operator

Mr and Mrs O'Brien have both moved out of the jobs they originally trained for. Mrs O'Brien is a trained hairdresser, but now works as an operator in manufacturing. Her husband started out in the shipbuilding industry, but was made redundant and took a position as a moulder in light manufacturing for a few years. 'It was very poorly paid' he commented, 'but what can you do? It was a job at the time'. Mr O'Brien had been out of work for six months at the time of the interview, on invalidity benefit but seeking suitable work. He had left work due to a heart attack (aged 45), and whilst his job had been kept open for him for nine months, his doctor had eventually advised against returning.

Mrs O'Brien had originally returned to work to pay for an extension on the house when their daughter (now 22) was a year and a half old, taking a job on the twilight shift so that her husband could be with the children. She has been in her current job, as an operator making units at a branch plant of a large electrical multinational company, for 13 years. She works 20 hours a week, on the twilight shift, leaving the house at 5.10 p.m. and returning at 9.35 p.m. Now that he is out of work, 'Carol is company', says her husband, 'if she was at work all day, I think you'd go out of your mind'.

Earning £3.30 take-home pay (1986 prices), Mrs O'Brien is the best-paid wife in the sample. 'I'm staying in my job because it's so well-paid', she says, pointing out that since she earns both bonus and a shift allowance, she would only earn £20 a week more if she worked full-time. 'The rate of pay during the day is disgraceful', remarks Mrs O'Brien, though she feels that she would not mind full-time work if it was in a wool shop or a children's department, both of which she would enjoy. Both Mr and Mrs O'Brien refer to their financial worries now that he is no longer working, though both their daughter and son (aged 18) are in full-time work, and make a contribution to their own keep. Mrs O'Brien mentioned the fact that she was poorly for over a year due to the chemicals at work, but that when her husband took ill she could not afford to leave.

She has since been moved to a separate department where she has been working for the past 2 years, and it is apparent from the description of her work routines that Mrs O'Brien has a strong pride in her work. Three 'girls' run four machines between them. (There has been some speed-up, since they used to run only two.) Every 3 weeks they take it in turns to act as 'wire man'. This involves a week of fetching reels of wire from the stores, operating an electric crane and a fork lift truck, pushing trucks loaded with wire, and dismantling pallets. As Mrs O'Brien remarks, its 'very, very heavy work – actually its killing', so whilst she likes her work, she feels that she could not manage this aspect of the job on a full-time basis.

Mr and Mrs Carrick: operator and home help

Prior to being made redundant, Mr Carrick had worked at the Royal Ordanance factory as an operator for something under 5 years. He qualified for redundancy pay, but since he had been unemployed for 4 years at the time of the interview, he was then on supplementary benefit. Mr Carrick is very clear that he is not a handy person, but besides pointing out that he does not have the appropriate skills to undertake casual work, he felt strongly that those of his mates who 'fiddle' are taking risks. He acknowledges that he has loads of free time, but 'I'm not bored, though I'd go mad if I didn't read'.

The Carricks have three children, all adults now, the eldest of whom is a staff nurse and has her own flat ('there's no rancour there'), whilst the second daughter and their son lived at home and are currently unemployed. Mrs Carrick had returned to work when their youngest was 5 years old 'because the children were old enough then'. After a few months, she obtained her current post as a home help, which she has held for the past 12 years, doing approximately 18 hours a week. Five of the thirty women in the sample were home helps, and it was apparent that Mrs Carrick, in common with others, loved her job. Being a home help 'isn't what it used to be. It isn't just cleaning', she points out. She sees the best part of her job as seeing to a schizophrenic lady's meals, who could not have managed without her, and though she does not enjoy ironing, 'it has to be done'. Mrs Carrick is well aware that the £40 she earns each week is 'taken off my husband's money in a sense, but I don't mind that'. She would not consider giving up work. For his part, Mr. Carrick is proud that his wife is so well-thought of in her job: 'everyone, from supervisors to clients sees Mrs Carrick as an excellent home help'.

Mr and Mrs Hogg: shipbuilding engineer and school dinner lady

The Hoggs were the oldest couple in the sample, and though both were below retiring age at the time of the interview, Mr Hogg (aged 63) had taken redundancy from the shipyards and retired early on invalidity benefit three years previously, while Mrs Hogg (60 years old) was about to retire early from her post as a school dinner lady. Their only son (in his mid thirties) lives with them and is a full-time quality controller in a United States controlled process manufacturing branch plant.

Mr Hogg was amongst the ten husbands who had worked in the shipbuilding industry and was one of the best paid of the men in the sample. He saw himself as one of the lucky ones in the inter-war depression, getting an apprenticeship in the shipbuilding industry in 1935. He left his first job in 1949 'for more experience', and spent the last 33 years of his working life with Doxfords involved in the installation of engines and auxilliaries. 'Two jobs: that was my life'. His work included going out on sea trials each month, and Mr Hogg had travelled to Germany, Holland, and other countries, on standby or for guarantee repairs on the larger ships that Doxfords used to fit out and test. He described himself as 'working round the clock', for 'if something happened you'd be out there 24 hours instead of 12'. 'He used to just come in and say, "pack a bag"' said his wife, 'he worked so many hours, our son used to ask if he had a daddy'.

Doxford Engines is a subsidiary of British Shipbuilding, and has been run down substantially from its mid 1970s employment of 1,100. In the spring of 1980 British Shipbuilders announced an end to over 100 years of engine-building at the plant, and around 500 men were made redundant. The remaining workforce of 250 were concentrated on making spare parts for the thousand or so existing Doxford engines and for the Sulzer engines made under licence at Clark Hawthorn's. There was a further bout of rationalisation in engine-building in mid 1984, new engine developments being concentrated at Clark Hawthorn's on the Tyne, and even the production of spare parts ceasing at the Doxford plant. Only a consultancy division employing eighty people remained (Stone and Stevens 1985).

In 1982, Mr Hogg had a nasty accident with his leg at work, and his consultant advised him that besides having a cartilege out, the accident had accelerated an arthritic condition. (No less than five men in the sample had suffered from work or unemployment-related illnesses, including two accidents, two cases of severe stress and one of serious depression. In other cases, including that of Mr O'Brien, the dividing line between sickness and unemployment was not easy to draw.) At the same time British Shipbuilders were calling for redundancies, and as Mrs Hogg put it 'the hours were becoming too long for him'. Having calculated the costs and benefits carefully, it become apparent that Mr Hogg would be better off to take the redundancy pay, particularly since he would be entitled to invalidity benefit, and to a pension from British Shipbuilders. The couple have been amongst the most fortunate in the sample, for, as Mrs Hogg pointed out 'we've never found it's reduced our living standards'. It should be mentioned that their son not only pays his board, but brings extras into the house as well.

Mrs Hogg has held her job on school dinners for 16 years. She had previously had her own business, running an off-licence for 2 years. When the premises were pulled down she found herself bored, so looked for other work. 'I was out of my tiny mind.' Mrs Hogg works 7½ hours a week, likes her job and 'loves the kids'. Her husband said that they had had forty extra Christmas cards thanks to her work, many of them hand made, and that when his wife had been in bed recently after an accident at school, the door bell had never stopped ringing. Mrs Hogg keeps all of her earnings, using them to buy tights and shoes, with the rest for holiday spending. 'I love spending money'. She plans to give up work at the end of the year, because going outside in the winter is getting too much, but feels that a younger person would not do her job because it would not be enough money. 'Me, it's pocket money.'

Chapter 2

The gender and spatial impact of structural economic change

A theoretical framework

Commentators have been remarking on the 'de-industrialisation' involved in the decline of employment in manufacturing in the developed industrialised economies for some time now. This has often been interpreted in terms of the rise of a 'service economy'. More recently there has been a growing awareness of the gender dimension to this structural economic change, with men losing full-time jobs in manufacturing and women taking part-time jobs in the service sector. However, as Dex (1987) points out, gender has not been integrated into explanations of de-industrialisation and economic restructuring. As this chapter unfolds, it will become apparent that the scale of the gender changes that have accompanied, and been part of other structural changes in the work process do indeed make it surprising that gender has not been an integral part of the analysis of these phenomena. It will also become clear that it is two-parent, working-class families who have been most severely affected, and it is the effect of economic restructuring on the household labour process of this group in particular that is the focus of the research underlying this book.

The overall aim of the chapter is to specify the problems of remaining within a traditional model of the gender division of labour market and domestic roles given the dramatic changes that have taken place in the gender patterns of employment and unemployment on both a national and a regional scale. Setting the scene has just given a flavour of the effects of such changes on individual families on Wearside, but to understand the social implications of changing employment patterns it is necessary to grasp how the process of industrial and economic restructuring affects class and gender structures. I propose to view structural change in the light of a particular theoretical framework: that of the changing patterns of accumulation of capital and of the reproduction of labour and capital within the capitalist world economy. In the context of long-wave changes, it is possible to analyse the factors underlying both the long post-war boom and the factors making for its demise. Using this approach, changing patterns in the employment structure can be integrated with these other changes, not just at a national level, but also at a regional one.

Let us look briefly at the elements of a theoretical framework for understanding how structural economic change is taking place and for linking it with changing employment patterns and the restructuring of work, before looking in more detail at the three major periods in post-war Britain: the long boom, the lower growth rates, and relative economic stagnation since 1972, with the period 1966 to 1971 as one of transition. Such a periodisation of post-war history is itself reliant upon long-wave theory, initially propounded by Kondratieff, but used since by a range of analysts, who have seen different forces at work in determining the transition between each quarter century or so of boom and recession. For Mandel (1975), it is changes in the profit rate that are crucial, while Armstrong, Glyn, and Harrison (1984) see the transition to recession as a crisis of over-accumulation of capital. A neo-Schumpetarian interpretation of the post-war boom would see the simultaneous explosive growth of several new technologies as the most convincing cause. Freeman, Clarke, and Soete (1982) put forward the concept of 'new technology systems' in which they see the technical and social interrelatedness of families of innovations. Yet others see the importance of changes in the capitalist labour process: for Dunford and Perrons (1983) technology is merely one component of change, which will also be put into effect through new principles of work organisation. Marshall (1987) advocates an eclectic use of long-wave theory, and this is the most useful for our purposes here.

> A major strength of the long-wave thesis is its capacity to merge a range of perspectives which focus upon isolated elements of capitalist development, such as technical change and the labour process or crisis tendencies and business cycles, to show how they impinge on one another and present them within a unified historical framework.

> (Ibid.:226)

A second useful analytical framework is Aglietta's theory of capitalist regulation (Aglietta 1979). For Aglietta a dynamic system must have a logic of internal transformation, and the question then arises as to how the system is regulated. He argues that the nodal point of the theory of capitalist regulation is the articulation of the laws of capital accumulation and the laws of competition, which requires elucidation of the contradictory process of the generalisation of the wage relation and the stratification of the two polar social classes. Aglietta argues that post-war prosperity was based on a system of monopolistic regulation relying on a process of intensive accumulation. This involved raising the rate of relative surplus value by the application of Taylor's principles of scientific management and emphasis on the production of goods for which economies of scale were possible, both of which meant a sustained rise in the productivity of labour, with a consequent renewal of the opportunities for investment. By the early 1970s the regime of intensive accumulation had come to an end. This was a function on the one hand of an increasing technical rigidity of the machine system with investment on a colossal scale, which required the expansion of markets, and on the other of a class struggle within the labour process. Capital responded to this with new forms of internationalisation, and with neo-Fordist techniques of control over the labour process, made possible by the more flexible mechanisation of micro-technology. The end of the regime of intensive accumulation was at one and the same time both a cause and a reflection of the destruction of the post-war international economic order based on United States hegemony (Aglietta 1982).

Finally, no analytical framework would be complete without an awareness that changing patterns of production affect consumption patterns as well as employment patterns, and that consumption in turn influences production. Intensive accumulation in the post-war period went along with a transformation of the conditions of existence of the wage-earning class and of the mode of consumption of Fordism. There are several views of the effect of the changing patterns of consumption on the domestic economy. There is first the perception that the growth of mass consumption and the 'commodification' – an awkward term, which implies the extension of the purchase of commodities on the market – this entails, means the progressive displacement of the family as a unit of production and its increasing importance as a unit of consumption. Women entering the labour market are significant in demand terms in that they boost family incomes and purchase labour-saving consumer durables. Gershuny (1978), in contrast, argues that the growth of the 'service economy', which seems to be part and parcel of changing consumption patterns, is more accurately the expansion of a 'self-service' economy. Households purchase consumer durables and undertake the service function of, say, washing, at home, using a washing machine, instead of going out to the launderette. Such an argument runs counter to the commodification argument. Gershuny's model of socio-technical innovation (briefly, the use of capital goods in the household, rather than the purchase of their services in the market) is useful in that it links the household in to the process of accumulation, though Gershuny himself does not examine the gender implications of his model.

To understand the nature and processes of development of industrial societies we must look outside 'the economy'. We must look at the 'informal economy', which is . . . an integral part of the system by which work, paid and unpaid, satisfies human needs.

(Gershuny 1985:129)

Such a model is obviously of considerable relevance to the project of this book, in linking changing employment patterns with household work strategies. It is also noticeable that the concept of socio-technical innovation fits into the long-wave thesis, as part of the post-war cluster of innovations.

Structural change during the long boom: 1945–66

In general terms, the years between the end of the war and the mid 1960s can be seen as a period of intensive accumulation, during which mass consumption emerged as a corollary of mass production. The long boom itself can however be divided into sub-periods, and in many ways the period of reconstruction from 1945 to 1952 follows a rather different pattern from the rest, for as Dunford and Perrons (1986) point out, it was manufacturing industry which expanded fastest at this time. As well as the expansion of new industries, reliance was placed on increasing output from Britain's older, nineteenth century industries, since this made use of existing capacity. By 1950 Britain was a highly specialised workshop economy, importing food and raw materials (including oil) and exporting manufactured exports.

The pattern of the 1950s extended the process of structural change initiated in the inter-war years. Cars and electrical and mechanical engineering played a key role in the process of economic growth. On the other hand, the older sectors, accounting for a substantial proportion of output and employment, grew only slowly. The static picture in Britain's nineteenth century industries was however overshadowed by the rapid expansion of other sectors of the economy. The 1950s saw the simultaneous explosive growth of several new technologies, involving first electrical engineering, including electrical consumer goods, telecommunications, the electrification of the railways, and the development of new weapons systems; and second chemicals, coal, and petroleum products and rubber and plastics. Such sustained expansion generated labour shortages, and demand for unskilled labour in particular became very strong. It is not surprising therefore, that under the economic circumstances of the 1950s with its labour shortages, particularly married women, as well as immigrants, should be drawn into employment. This was not, however at the expense of male employment.

This then, was a period with an intensive regime of accumulation in which Fordism and Taylorism were being applied, albeit not as fully in Britain as elsewhere. The Fordist technological paradigm of high volume production of standardised products was associated with changes in work organisation. Taylorist principles allowed of increased production and increased management control, but also involved the social costs of intensification of the segmentation of the labour market and more standardised, simplified, and repetitive jobs. Such increased division of labour created jobs which were seen as particularly suited to women: detailed and repetitive tasks were 'women's work'. The evolution of the social division of labour in the manufacturing and industrial sectors thus reinforced labour shortage factors in encouraging women into the labour force as a reserve army of labour. Labour market segmentation was, in fact, something that was highly characteristic of women's employment, so that by the 1960s the concentration of women in a few, low-paid occupations had become marked.

The 1950s were also the years during which mass consumption emerged as a corollary of mass production. There were two interacting ways in which this occurred. First, there was direct economic compulsion on wage earners to purchase certain additional commodities and services. On the one hand, the new kinds of production and work involved in Taylorism–Fordism increased the intensity of work, and a higher level of consumption became necessary to restore energy and strength. On the other hand, 'the increasing extension of the capitalist conurbations lengthens the circulation time between home and work to such an extent that time-saving consumer goods likewise become a condition for the actual reconstitution of labour power.' (Mandel 1975: 394) As Dunford and Perrons (1983) point out, individual commodity consumption of such a nature is best suited to consumption in a compact space of time and at a single place, the home. The structure of the post-war consumption norm was thus governed by standardised housing as the site for individual consumption, and by the motor car as the mode of transport compatible with the separation of work and home. This opened the way for the household to become a substantial centre of investment in consumer durable goods.

Second, this was a period in which the wage relation was generalised, or as Mingione (1985) suggests, high rates of accumulation were being combined with high rates of commodification, meaning that more and more goods were being purchased on the market for money. There was a reduction of food costs, combined with rising real wages – wages being linked with productivity and the cost of living – and with married women going out to work, thus increasing incomes. This meant that families were also in a position to purchase additional commodities.

During the early 1960s, as Aglietta would see it, a general crisis of Fordism had begun to develop as a function of the increasing technical rigidity of the machine system, with investment on a colossal scale, which required continuing expansion of markets. There was also a growing class struggle within the labour process (Glynn and Sutcliffe 1972), and as the relative costs of labour changed, the emphasis of investment shifted from simple capacity extension to 'rationalisation' and cost-cutting. The long-term response of capital was to make use of new forms of internationalisation and to introduce neo-Fordist methods of work organisation in the 1970s. Meanwhile, the shift to cost-cutting that occurred in the first half of the 1960s meant that women continued to be drawn in to the labour market, though increasingly on a part-time basis, and, as we shall see in later sections of the chapter, particularly on a decentralised basis at the regional periphery.

A final feature of structural economic change which had become clear by the middle of the 1960s was the growth in service employment. The service sector of the economy was of course one in which women were extensively employed. Bell (1974), in a reformulation of Engels' law, argued that economic development involved a shift in household expenditure from basic necessities to luxuries, so that as people get richer they demand more personal services. Criticising Bell, Gershuny (1978) distinguishes the undoubtedly substantial growth in service employment from the final demand for services. He shows that expenditure on marketed services actually fell as a proportion of income over the post-war period, whilst that on manufactured products rose. To explain his data, Gershuny argues that Engels' law fails to take account of technological change and points to a series of post-war socio-technical innovations which have allowed the rise of a self-service economy. If one distinguishes the demand for the final service function and the demand for services, it becomes clear that capital investment is now taking place on a large scale in households, and that consumer durables, which maintain the market for manufactured products, allow households to replace marketed services with services they provide themselves.

A period of transition: 1966–71

The period from 1966 to 1971 saw on opening-up of crisis at the international level in the regime of accumulation, which was experienced with particular severity in Britain due to the decline in national competitiveness, and this led

> to an accelerated rationalisation and restructuring of many of the
> leading sectors that had played a role in the preceding wave of

expansion, while the slackening of the process of growth and of increases in real incomes eventually led to reductions in orders for many branches of production and to the appearances of substantial amounts of excess capacity in many sectors.

(Dunford and Perrons 1986:92)

To understand the changing structure of employment in Britain at this time, as well as in the period of slow growth since 1972, it is important to grasp both the major features of the impending international crisis and the way in which these interacted with specifically British problems.

Let us look at the transition taking place at the international level first of all, which has been interpreted in a number of ways. Following Aglietta's analysis, this was the period at which the regime of intensive accumulation which had characterised the long post-war boom began to come to an end. This was due to a mounting crisis within the Fordist labour process, with difficulties in extending Fordism further. As reserves of labour declined within the developed capitalist economies, wage costs were rising, and, in addition, limits to the extension of economies of scale were becoming apparent. Whilst technical change continued to occur at a high rate, products tended to vary, and since markets were also tending to stagnate, the simple extension of mass production was no longer on the cards. Capital was forced to adopt new strategies in order to maintain profit rates.

In the first place, increasing wage costs in the developed economies encouraged western capital to seek new locations for production where labour costs were cheaper, namely in parts of the Third World. By the beginning of the 1970s the 'new international division of labour' was an observable phenomenon, with new manufacturing facilities being established in the Newly Industrialising Countries. The old vertical division of labour between raw material producers and manufacturing countries, established during the colonial era, was giving way to a horizontal division of labour in which both developed and at least some developing countries were involved in manufacturing. By the beginning of the new decade, it was no longer possible to shift the contradictions arising from the long boom to the developing countries where the surplus unemployed population simply expanded to absorb them. It was becoming the turn of the developed counties to experience unemployment as well, though, in the first instance at least, the new international division of labour only tended to affect male manufacturing jobs.

The second strategy which capital began to adopt to maintain profit rates at this juncture, involved neo-Fordist strategies for the organisation of work within the developed economies themselves. Neo-Fordism reversed the fragmentation of the labour process initiated by Fordism and allowed the reintegration of work roles within the enterprise. This was because technological developments were opening the door to flexible forms of mechanisation which weakened the link between mechanisation and scale. Organisational changes which tended to favour the adoption of work roles began to be possible, instead of Fordist individual repetitive tasks performed on a hierarchical basis. Neo-Fordism meant a reconstitution of the labour process with a re-centralisation and re-skilling of sectors of the workforce. However, these changes in the labour process meant that a further polarisation and segmentation of jobs in the labour market was superimposed on an already existent labour market segmentation, with its hierarchy of skills, pay, security, status, and power. Since one of the major dimensions of labour market segmentation was in any case gender, with women concentrated in low grade and low-paid jobs, neo-Fordism was likely to strengthen gender divisions within the labour market still further.

As Aglietta (1982) emphasises, this was also a period in which the cohesion to the international economic order, provided by United States hegemony since Bretton Woods, began to break up. By the beginning of the 1970s the destruction of the post-war economic order was well under way. Aglietta argues that there is no tendency for international harmonisation via the homogenisation of nations, so that hegemony is a principal form of cohesion between nations. The period up to 1970 certainly saw a relative eclipse of United States domination of the western world economy, as its share of world output dropped (Armstrong, Glyn, and Harrison 1984). At the same time, several factors were undermining the post-war international economic order (Aglietta 1982). Inflation in the United States was undermining the dollar, and the convergence of national industrial structures and the loss of United States supremacy contributed to the difficulties. Japan had not followed the new international division of labour pattern of other advanced economies, and so was able to become a global power through exports of manufactures without laying open its own markets to imports, and this was undermining the stability of international trade. The international debt economy had also become relatively immune from regulation due to the collapse of the dollar's functions. The rise in oil rents in 1973 gave the final blow to the old cohesion, and the world economy moved decisively into an extended period of relative economic stagnation and recession.

During the later 1960s and early 1970s, some specifically British weaknesses interacted with the international forces just described, ensuring that the transition from the long boom was peculiarly problematic for the United Kingdom's economy. As early as the period 1966 to 1971, manufacturing employment as a whole fell. First, whilst we have already pointed out that at an international level, there was a crisis of the Fordist mode of accumulation, in Britain this was superimposed on the fact that the country had never fully adopted Fordist norms of production (Dunford, Gedes, and Perrons 1981). Thus although British industry had imported American labour process techniques, the United Kingdom did not develop the large scale standardised production processes necessary for international competitiveness in the period up to 1966. This was partly due to the domestic market being neither large enough nor stable enough, but also to rigidities in labour supply. It was particularly the well-organised working-class that contributed to these rigidities: trade unions had a high degree of job control, which impeded the introduction of new technology, whilst wages had a high share of value added.

Additional features of a peculiarly British dimension, are the much commented upon separation of industrial and financial capital in the United Kingdom and the fact that political priority was given to the financial function, involving interest and exchange rate policies that were often detrimental to industry. In addition, British public resources tended to be directed to welfare and armaments, and not to planned investment in manufacturing industry, as in the case of some of her competitors. Finally, as Dunford and Perrons (1986) put it: 'an external constraint reinforced the problems posed by the structure of the industrial system and by the internal conditions of surplus production on which its growing backwardness as a capitalist system lay' (Dunford and Perrons 1986:76–7). Whilst during the late nineteenth century British industry had the advantage of being based within the dominant imperialist power, 'by the 1960s British capitalism had long since lost that position and became, in turn, subordinate to an international pattern of trade and monetary circulation centring upon the dominance of the USA' (Marshall 1987:203–4). Britain was thus particularly poorly placed with respect to the international changes that went along with the relative decline of American hegemony.

From 1966, then, there are a number of new features present in the British economy, which relate particularly to a marked change in the performance of British manufacturing industry. Excess capacity became endemic within the manufacturing sector. The decline of manufacturing was apparent in quantitative changes which took place around this time too. Whilst between 1955 and 1966 manufacturing employment in Britain had grown more slowly than any other advanced capitalist country, between 1966 and 1973 it fell more than any other country apart from Sweden, and at an annual average rate of 1.2 per cent (Rowthorn 1986). This employment decline was largely associated with technical change, since modernisation had led to 'jobless growth' (Massey and Meegan 1982).

However, qualitative changes in the ownership and control, technical organisation, and spatial distribution of manufacturing were perhaps of

41

greater importance than quantitative ones. Britain, in other words, experienced not merely a decline of manufacturing industry, but also a process of industrial restructuring. The pattern of ownership and control of British industry was extensively altered by the merger and take over movement of the end of the 1960s, which involved the transfer to acquiring companies of 20 per cent of total net assets in manufacturing.

Others sought cheaper conditions of production by means of a spatial redistribution, to which we shall return in later sections of this chapter. 'The geographical reorganisation of British capital within Britain (as well as externally) was an important element in its early response to impending crisis' (Massey 1986:37). At an international level, American capital had been consolidating its base in the United Kingdom during the long boom, so that by 1966, American companies owned 7.2 per cent of the net capital stock in Britain and accounted for over a tenth of total manufacturing sales (Marshall 1987:209). Meanwhile, British multinationals were tending to defer domestic investment for decentralisation abroad, and direct investment abroad by British firms grew substantially during the 1960s. These growing international movements of capital were associated with the accelerated restructuring of the network of capital ownership and control in the domestic merger wave.

What was the effect of all these changes on the structure of employment? The proportion of women in the labour force continued to rise over this period. This was not, however, a result of the absolute decline in the number of men employed, but rather a function of the fact that women were concentrated in expanding sectors of the economy such as services, sectors which were at the same time, labour-intensive. It is nevertheless important to be aware that women continued to be concentrated in low-paid industries and occupations. Virtually three-quarters of the women in the labour force in 1971 remained in a mere thirteen occupations, all defined as women's work, a decline of only about 5 per cent on the figures for 1961 and 1951 (Henwood and Wyatt 1986:123). An indicator of women's low pay is that 86 per cent of char workers were women in 1971. Amongst academic commentators, these features were recognised as labour market segmentation.

International restructuring and British de-industrialisation: 1971–today

During the 1970s, the regime of intensive accumulation came to an end, with two oil shocks contributing to the difficulties already being experienced by the international economy. Slow growth and high unemployment had become hallmarks of the world economy, and over-accumulation and the expansion of surplus production meant insufficient commodification and strong over-production. In Britain, the combination of these international factors with specifically British weaknesses, meant that relative job decline in manufacturing became absolute job decline. Manufacturing employment fell at an average rate of 3.1 per cent per annum between 1973 and 1983, a greater rate than any other industrialised country besides Belgium. Industrial employment had been at its peak in 1966, providing 11.5 million jobs; by 1984 it had fallen to less than 7 million. Manufacturing employment alone stood at 8.7 million in 1966, and had fallen to 5.4 million by 1984, with about half of that loss occurring after 1979 (Rowthorn 1986). In addition, it is remarkable that the British decline in manufacturing employment was sustained over virtually the whole of the manufacturing sector.

By the beginning of the 1970s, rationalisation and intensification within manufacturing was being systemically extended to an international scale Britain's role as an exporter of capital made her singularly well-placed to take advantage of the new international division of labour, and job loss in industry was no longer simply a product of domestic structural adjustment, but of abandonment by national capitals of domestic industrial production. The result was major losses of male jobs in manufacturing industry from the beginning of the 1970s, with a wholesale route from the end of the decade. Male manual jobs were the subject of an additional squeeze, in that there was a continuing trend towards administration in manufacturing industry.

Several factors made for the continuing buoyancy of women's employment, despite the difficulties being experienced by men. First, neo-Fordist management strategies continued to draw women into the labour force, whilst at the same time tending to discard men, since neo-Fordist techniques for cutting costs required more flexibility on the part of the labour force. What had already been observed by academics in terms of women being found predominantly in the secondary, segmented labour market, was experienced by employers as precisely this required flexibility. For female employees, flexibility was built in, first in terms of higher turnover rates, as they left the labour market for domestic reasons, and second because so many of them were part-time anyway. It is indeed true, of course, that women lost jobs in manufacturing as well as men, and indeed at a greater rate, but men lost a far greater absolute number of jobs.

A second factor benefiting women was the continuing growth of the service sector, although the growth of services during this period is a complex phenomenon. True, the share of services as a whole in employment rose over this period, continuing the trend of earlier periods. During the 1970s, however, it was primarily the state's expanding social expenditure which drew women in to employment, in the National Health Service, in education and in social services. The fiscal crisis of the state, which began to be apparent under the Labour government, slowed down this process of expansion for women's employment. Private, non-producer services continued to expand during the 1970s but with the cut backs in state expenditure in the 1980s, private services became relatively more buoyant. Again, it tended to be women who were drawn into private sector services too. Why should the service sector have provided buoyancy for specifically women's employment? Essentially because, unlike manufacturing, the only possibilities for cost savings in the service sector arose from employing cheaper labour. In manufacturing, technical innovation, which had led to jobless growth during the 1960s, continued during the 1970s, making services relatively more labour intensive. Unlike manufacturing, services were not, on the whole, subject to international competition either. Services could only trim costs by employing low-paid women, especially on a part-time basis.

In summary, for the period between the end of the Second World War and 1971, the rise in the proportion of women workers does not appear to be at the expense of men. What is different about the gender structure of employment from 1971 onwards, is that women's employment increased, whilst men's decreased. In the thirty years from 1951 to 1971 women's employment increased by nearly 2 million, but men's employment declined by less than 300,000. In contrast, in only a decade between 1971 and 1981, women's employment increased by nearly 300,000 whilst men's fell by 3.1 million. The rise in the proportion of female employees was the result of an absolute decline in the number of males (Henwood and Wyatt 1986). So whilst female participation rates have increased continually since the Second World War, men's participation rates have suffered a dramatic decline since the beginning of the 1970s. Women were drawn into the labour force during the long boom as a 'reserve army of labour', but the pattern continued in recession for reasons of cheapness.

This picture, however, needs to be modified by the realisation that the shift from manufacturing to services also involved a continuation of the trend in the composition of employment away from full-time male and towards part-time female employment. There were substantial increases in the share of part-time employment amongst women over the decade between 1971 and 1981, rising from 33.5 per cent of female employment to 41.6 per cent. The factors encouraging the growth of part-time employment since 1971 have already been discussed in terms of neo-Fordist flexibility. It is also important to realise that the occupational segregation of women has continued since 1971 as well. In other words, whilst there is an issue of the *quantity* of employment available, particularly for male manual workers, the changing employment structure of the 1970s raised the question of the *quality* of work available for women. Better-paid, male jobs were being lost, whilst lower-paid, part-time female jobs were being substituted.

As Britain has moved into the 1980s, it is possible to suggest that features that were formerly chiefly in evidence in women's labour market experiences are now becoming part of male labour market experience as well. The rationalisation process which had been part of firms' responses to the squeeze on profitability has continued, but a further strategy has been added, that of the intensification of work. This has been achieved by increasing the segmentation of labour markets *within* firms. Employers are reorganising their 'manpower' (*sic*) systems into primary, core, and variable, peripheral components. Godfrey (1986) argues that the internal labour market of many firms is fragmenting into 'increasingly peripheral, and hence numerically variable, groups of workers, clustered around a numerically stable core group of employees, responsible for the key, firm-specific activities of the organization.' (ibid.:229) Commentators have been talking increasingly of the 'flexible firm' and of 'flexible workers'. Whilst it remains true that the majority of temporary and part-time workers in the 1980s are still women, work-intensification and the move to flexibility mean that men may become increasingly subject to the low pay and insecurity which has tended to characterise female employment to date.

It is worth noting in this context too, that self-employment has risen substantially over the recent period. Self-employment shows significant features of flexibility in that it is often low-paid and insecure. Whilst rates of increase for self-employed women are higher than those for men, men still make up by far the greater part of the self-employed. On the other hand, prospects for female employment are not good either; women are being squeezed both by the rolling back of the state and by technological change in the service sector.

Unemployment, social recomposition, and gender roles in post-war Britain

The process of industrial restructuring described in the previous sections has involved a parallel process of social recomposition, or class restructuring. Post-war changes in the structure of employment are also reflected in parallel changes in the patterns of unemployment, and the steady growth in unemployment since the beginning of the 1970s, together with its dramatic rate of increase from the middle of that decade, are well-known phenomena. Changing levels of unemployment have also involved changes in its social composition. This section is concerned to highlight the process of social recomposition and its effects on gender roles, first with regard to unemployment and then with regard to employment.

As a starting point, it is important to be aware of the implications of the changing structure of employment for the framework of state policies towards unemployment. This framework was devised before the end of the last war by Beveridge and Keynes, who can be seen as the two chief architects of the 'liberal collectivism' which laid the foundations for the post-war social democratic consensus which held sway until the 1970s. Both Keynes and Beveridge saw economic and social problems as caused by limited and remediable malfunctions of the market system. However, both men made crucial assumptions about the *composition* as well as the level of employment, and whilst their assumptions about level were more or less fulfilled, those on composition certainly were not. 'The crucial economic premise was that, at least in respect of male employment, there would not be a problem of *low* wages deriving from the composition of employment' (Cutler, Williams, and Williams 1986:65). In other words, Beveridge built the state benefit system around the concept of the male breadwinner, whilst Keynes did not imagine that reflation would have to confront increased activity drawing in more lower-paid part-time female workers. It was no wonder that a policy crisis arose during the 1970s; a crisis of Keynesianism on the one hand and a fiscal crisis of the state on the other.

J. W. C. Cumes (1984) takes these implications a step further, and argues that, given the institutional constraints arising from the structure of employment in developed countries – due in part, as we shall see, to gender patterns – policies of Keynesian stabilisation unintentionally promote international restructuring in a process which is hard to reverse. Cumes argues that social expenditure rose dramatically in all the developed capitalist economies during the 1950s, partly as a component of the implementation of Keynesian policies, and partly for their own intrinsic value. But by the end of the 1960s, the capacity and will to move consumption and investment both together, up and down, as Keynesian fine-tuning demanded, had passed. This was particularly because consumption had become relatively inflexible. High-consumption unemployment became institutionalised.

Amongst several factors contributing to this state of affairs was the fact that the single breadwinner phenomenon was being eroded by married women working, so that unemployment became less destructive of family incomes, and it was savings rather than consumption that suffered from lower incomes. When governments tried to move the economy down, they thus acted only on production and investment, not on consumption. This intensified the pressure of consumption demand and thus of inflation, precisely the opposite of what was intended by Keynesian demand management. Indeed, Cumes argues, aggregate demand now tends not to fall even in periods of recession. Downward movement in Western economies is only in investment and production, which means that Newly Industrialised Countries especially find a buoyant market for their products even in 'recession'. On the other hand, domestic producers in developed countries lose market shares as imports flow in to satisfy shortages of supply created by the reduction of domestic production.

The institutionalisation of high-consumption unemployment during the 1960s has thus interacted with state policies aimed at reducing unemployment in the 1970s to reinforce de-industrialisation in the developed economies. Ironically, policies of stabilisation have also contributed to the rising crisis, both of the state, and of the economy. Increases in total employment, particularly of married women, have been offset by rises in unemployment. This means that production increases have been offset by social expenditures, with a corresponding tendency for the state to move towards fiscal crisis. State benefits for the unemployed also effectively mean that the state is subsidising consumption during periods of unemployment. This allows relative over-commodification in certain consumer durables to subsist alongside overpopulation, contributing to the instability of the system (Mingione 1985).

Just as changing patterns of employment and unemployment affect the interaction between state policies towards unemployment and economic structures, so do they also affect the significance of unemployment figures themselves. Gender is frequently an important aspect of this significance. The rate of unemployment can now be deceptive owing to the entry of women, part-timers, and casual workers into the work force. Rising unemployment can go with an increase in total employment, something which has actually happened. In Britain, between 1973 and 1979, the number of new jobs created was less than half the increase in the labour force, so that unemployment rates rose substantially (Ashton 1986). Between 1980 and 1984, the working population rose by about a quarter of a million, but over this period, employees in employment fell (by just over 1.5 million), the number of unemployed rose (by just under 1.5 million), but there was a large proportional rise in the number of employers and self-employed of over 300,000 (Cutler, Williams, and Williams 1986).

What of the changes in the social composition of unemployment that have taken place with the rise in unemployment? Two important factors mean that unemployment tends to be concentrated in the secondary labour market. The segmentation of the labour market into primary, secure, relatively well-paid jobs, and secondary, insecure, relatively poorly-paid, sectors; means that unemployment occurs in the latter. The second factor arises from institutional regulation of the labour market. In a comparison between the United States and Britain, Ashton (1986) suggests that the proportion of the British labour force with some form of job security is higher, thanks to union density, professional associations, the scope of collective bargaining, and of health and safety; so that unemployment is highly concentrated among the low paid.

Not merely does unemployment tend to fall on those sections of the labour market who are in any case low-paid, but unemployment lasting 3 months or more will produce a more or less permanent fall in grade, as well as affecting occupational pensions. In other words, state benefits do not protect the unemployed against the long-term effects on prospects, earnings, and occupational pensions (Hakim 1982). Rising unemployment means that the proportion who are long term unemployed also goes up. There are three groups particularly at risk from long-term unemployment. First, there are the young with a history of recurrent unemployment, especially the unskilled and the semi-skilled. Second, there are established workers, who fall straight from long-lasting jobs into long-term unemployment, and are generally older manual or white collar workers entering unemployment via redundancy or ill health. The final category are the occupationally downgraded, skilled individuals who have moved out of industries in long-term structural decline (Ashton 1986). The latter two categories feature highly in the sample used in my own empirical study. Despite the recent fall in the number of unemployed, there will undoubtedly be a lag in the fall of the long-term unemployed. Such a lag is a feature of the end of a recession, because job recruits are of those who are newly unemployed.

It would seem that in Britain at least, men experience more unemployment than women. Although men receive more state transfer payments than women, which ensure some cushioning against unemployment, there are still major long-term financial losses involved in unemployment. Substantial and long-term unemployment amongst men means that males are increasingly experiencing the broken labour market patterns that have been characteristic of women to date. However, whilst disrupted labour market patterns are the experience of most women; as one might expect from the changing patterns of employment spelled out in the previous section, unemployment is particularly concentrated amongst unskilled and skilled male manual workers. In other words, it is working-class men in particular whose labour market patterns are moving closer to those of women.

Let us now turn to an examination of the social recomposition of employment consequent upon the process of industrial restructuring described in previous sections. The major changes in the structure of employment that have taken place can be looked at in terms of three processes: feminisation of the labour market, its internationalisation and most recently its casualisation. The effect, as Cutler, Williams, and Williams (1986:87) point out, is that since the war there has been 'a secular change in the identity of the typical wage earner and in the sources of (as it used to be thought) his wages'. This change started during the long boom, when it was a matter of married women going out to work and contributing to the family income. It has continued with the recession of the 1970s, during which time men tended to lose jobs, whilst female employment continued to expand. It has also been a feature of such recovery as has been in evidence since the beginning of the 1980s, for it has become apparent that recovery has continued to draw in more lower-paid, part-time workers. In theory, the service jobs created for women are equivalent to the manufacturing jobs lost by men. But in fact, service jobs – with the exception of producer services, which have been subject to the same decline as manufacturing – are lower paid and tend to be part-time. The changes in the composition and level of employment have thus hit certain groups particularly severely. It is especially working-class two-parent families who have suffered from the collapse of the relatively well-paid manufacturing sector (Cutler, Williams, and Williams 1986).

What is the potential for changes in gender relations, both in the home and in paid work, resulting from the new employment patterns? If one takes the fairly widely-accepted feminist model, which sees the status of women in the labour market as the result of the interaction between the two social systems of patriarchy and capitalism, these changes threaten patriarchal structures, at the same time as being clearly of considerable importance to capitalism in its efforts to maintain profitability. 'In this situation of high *male* unemployment, the increasing participation of women in the labour market, if only on a part-time basis, threatens patriarchal structures and it is by no means clear how this conflict will be resolved' (Henwood and Wyatt 1986:109). And though Henwood and Wyatt do not mention this, the potential conflict between patriarchy and capitalism will become even greater if current restructuring continues to move in the direction of low wage competition, with women's flexibility being duplicated by lower wages and poorer conditions for men. Let us briefly consider the dimensions of the social restructuring of employment, and assess the extent to which they challenge traditional models of the gender division of labour.

First, whilst women's employment opportunities have risen steadily over the post-war period, manual male jobs particularly have been contracting. This undermines the traditional view of the husband as the economic provider for the family, the breadwinner, or less emotively, the worker-earner. On the other hand, the challenge to patriarchal perceptions is limited by the fact that women's employment has increasingly been part-time. The conditions under which state benefits are made available on the one hand encourage men to enter full-time unemployment, and on the other render it almost impossible for low-paid wives to use their earnings as a cushion against their husbands' unemployment. A second factor strengthening the relative economic position of women in the labour market is that the changing industry distribution of employment has meant that women have tended to find themselves in expanding sectors of the economy, whilst men have tended to be in contracting sectors. Again, however, the challenge to traditional stereotypes is limited, this time by women's concentration in lower-paid industries.

It is, however, occupation which is the primary determinant of whether an individual actually obtains employment. Here the gender picture of relative prospects for men and women is less clear. Male manual workers have obviously already suffered a substantial squeeze in terms of employment prospects. But female service workers are also under threat from a number of sources. The fiscal crisis of the state initially, then the rise of the New Right and cuts in public service provision, have already limited prospects in the public sector. Technological change now threatens employment in the service sector, both in the public and the private sectors. The effects of new technology are already apparent in the retail sector, and are coming into effect in clerical occupations too. These are of course areas in which female employment is concentrated. It is interesting to note that professional occupations are also now under threat from restructuring – growing unemployment amongst middle management for example – and from intensification. The extent to which this will feed through in terms of loss of employment potential amongst predominantly male professionals has yet to be seen.

But perhaps the most significant factor maintaining women's inferior economic status is their earnings. Average weekly earnings for women are three-fifths those of men; average hourly earnings two-thirds. There has been some improvement over the post-war period, particularly during the 1970s, assisted by the sex discrimination legislation, but the evidence suggests that progress has been eroded, at least in terms of hourly earnings, from the mid 1970s. There is the additional fact that in the 1980s much of women's employment is part-time, and that female part-time hourly earnings have deteriorated relative to female full-time earnings throughout the post-war period, though the comparison with male full-time earnings is more complex.

The extent to which the changing gender structure of employment is a challenge to a patriarchal social structure is thus ambivalent. Any simplified picture of 'women taking men's jobs' requires serious modification in the light of the major limitations on any growth in the economic power of women. Nevertheless, economic restructuring over the post-war period has brought substantial social restructuring in its train, with significant gender implications. It is apparent that many of the features of post-war structural economic change are coming together to reinforce a questioning as to the viability of the male breadwinner model, in particular feminisation of the workforce, and the continuing high volume of unemployment. Long-term unemployment, and the possibility that employers are shifting to more flexible patterns of employment only add to the problems of remaining within a traditional model of the gender division of labour market and domestic roles. The way in which state benefits are structured, however, does much to confirm the traditional model.

The contradiction between the state benefit system established by Beveridge and the changing gender structure of economic opportunity have already been looked at, but are spelled out in the criticisms made of the Beveridge framework by Ekins (1986). As he points out, many of the assumptions underlying Beveridge's thinking bear little relation to contemporary reality. This is particularly so with regard to gender aspects of employment and unemployment. First, paid employment is no longer an effective instrument for preventing financial poverty. The Low Pay Unit has shown that one third of the workforce in Britain suffers from low pay, and that additionally the majority of the low paid are women. Changing family structure has led to a dramatic increase in female-headed households, and such households are particularly subject to poverty.

Beveridge also assumed that a rigid formal employment structure of full-time work is the norm, that full employment for men during their working lives is desirable and feasible and that married women are, or wish to be, merely financial appendages of their husbands. As already spelled out in some detail, the growth of part-time work, of male unemployment and of the number of married women in paid work all contradict such assumptions. It is unclear how contradictions of such major proportions will be resolved. However, in the second part of the book, Chapters 4 and 5 will examine the extent to which the Wearside empirical study provides an indication of the effect of economic restructuring on the household labour process, and whether it has led to any challenge to patriarchal social structures within the household. It is therefore important to specify the regional impact of economic restructuring.

The spatial effects of economic restructuring: Wearside and the North East

The spatial dimensions to the economic restructuring process already described at the national level, add further force to the importance of the gender dimension in the parallel process of social recomposition. From the early 1960s to the late 1970s, the North East, in common with other

British regions, saw high rates of growth of female employment –
especially amongst the married, the part-time, and the unskilled – a
feature which coincided in the latter part of the period with a dramatic
fall in male unemployment. This has lately been interpreted in terms of
a 'North/South divide' within the British economy. Wearside, the
location for the empirical study, provides a particularly stark case of
such regional differentiation, where, as will be shown, the contraction of
manufacturing since 1979 has specially affected male employment
opportunities, as have the cutbacks in the public sector, including shipbuilding and coal mining; whilst the service sector is still providing
some buoyancy for women's jobs. The consideration of these spatial
dimensions will thus concentrate on the northern region in general, and
Wearside in particular.

Changing patterns of employment and unemployment in the regions
can be analysed within a similar theoretical framework to that used for
national changes in the first section of this chapter, and it will be seen
that the same periodisation contributes to an understanding of the
changing forces at work. It is nevertheless important to realise that there
are differences from the national picture, for as Marshall (1987) points
out, only a few regions have exhibited the classical pattern of a historical
succession of leading industrial sectors across the course of long waves.
Most regions, including the North, have been dominated by one or two
industries whose development has been confined to a single wave. Yet
the evolving regional hierarchy has entailed more than simply industrial
structural change; 'it has centred upon historical transformations in the
social division of labour and the evolution of the capitalist labour
process' (Marshall 1987:228).

The North East has been transformed over a long period from a
region occupying a pivotal position in the global accumulation process
to one that has become marginal to its main currents. Although it could
be argued that de-industrialisation has been going on for many decades
in the North East, relative decline has been accompanied by wide
fluctuations in absolute output and employment (Hudson 1986). Such
fluctuations are explicable in terms of uneven development in the heavy
industry sectors during economic fluctuations in the demand for their
output, with capital goods tending to overshoot in their response. The
growth of Empire and Britain's international dominance had created the
spatial structures which gave the North East its prosperity during the
nineteenth century, based on the growth of an inter-sectoral spatial
division of labour involving specialisation in coal, shipbuilding, and
steel. The decline of Britain's dominance was at the heart of the regional
problem of the inter-war years, a problem that was particularly clear in
the North East. However, in the immediate postwar period, there was a
national emphasis on exports from the basic industries inherited from

the nineteenth century. The difficulties of the North East had apparently receded.

It was during this period that the foundations were laid for the state to play a crucial role in the spatial problems of the region. The Labour government's nationalisation policy affected patterns of control over capital accumulation and employment in a particularly marked manner, taking into public control, the major industries of the North East. The decline of the coal industry began at the start of the 1950s, although employment decline in steel and shipbuilding began later, towards the end of the 1960s and 1970s respectively. Job loss – amounting to 200,000 jobs – in these three nationalised industries made up 80 per cent of the total net employment decline in the region in mining and manufacturing in the thirty years to 1981 (Hudson 1986). Perhaps as important in the long run, was the fact that nationalisation compensation allowed former owners to switch capital to more profitable activities and locations.

By 1959, the geography of British manufacturing employment was dominated by the big cities and by the central regions of the West Midlands and the South East: almost the mirror image of the old coal, steel, and shipbuilding complexes. In other words, there had been a continuation of the inter-war patterns of growth in sectors associated with mass consumption; and of the spatial division between regions specialising in consumption goods manufacture, and the older established raw materials/capital goods equipment production. Indeed, up until the mid-1960s, employment growth in the South East and the Midlands, and losses in the North can mainly be put down to structural factors meaning that there was a particular mix of industries in each region which tended to expand or contract in accordance with the aggregate trend of these industries at a national level.

In the North East, of course, decline at this time was associated not merely with manufacturing decline in the shipbuilding industry – a result of the change in position of the North East in the international division of labour – but also in primary production, thanks to the British state's decisions about using oil rather than coal as a primary energy source. From the end of the 1950s, extensive reserves of male and female labour were recreated in the region (Hudson 1986). In addition, by the beginning of the 1960s, labour had become quite strong in the central regions. Regional disparities in the demand and supply of labour were of course a function of the growing difficulties of the Fordist mode of accumulation, and decentralisation of production to the periphery was a major part of the early response to the need to trim costs as a way of maintaining profitability.

The period from the end of the 1950s to the middle of the 1960s, then, saw marked changes in the pattern of regional development in Britain, with decentralisation of manufacturing production as an early response by capital to the problems in the Fordist mode of accumulation. New manufacturing establishments at the periphery were usually branch plants of multinational companies. Enhanced financial incentives from state regional policies, as well as reserves of labour, encouraged such decentralisation. With regard to the North East, there was thus some diversification of the regional economy, but with little net growth, since there was also much restructuring of existing capacity, especially in chemicals. However, the type of employment provided was radically different. It was production operations and assembly work, involving unskilled or semi-skilled manual work or routine managerial work, that tended to be decentralised. In the North East, for example, this meant a movement from skilled or heavy manual work done by men on shifts to semi or unskilled routine assembly work done by married women (Hudson 1986).

Changes in the organisation and location of industry thus generated a demand for female labour, but this was a response to, and shaped by the spatial distribution of female labour reserves. The latter were a function of previous patterns of industry and employment, where the strict division of labour made women relatively inexperienced, 'green labour' and therefore cheap (Lewis 1983). This was the period during which female activity rates in the regions began to converge. Regions with initially low percentages of women paid workers, characterised either by heavy industry, or agriculture, or both as in the North, saw sharp increases in the proportion of women in the labour force. The rise of female activity rates was reinforced by the growth of the service sector and by the transfer of government offices to the periphery, both of which tended to involve routine office jobs (Henwood and Wyatt 1986).

The year 1966 can be seen as a watershed in spatial patterns of employment, marking the turning point from the expansionary post-war wave to relative economic stagnation. The decline of regional differences in industrial structure which were the result of the decentralising response to declining profitability, marked the beginning of a shift to a 'new spatial division of labour' (Massey 1979). The *inter*-sectoral divisions of labour originally laid down in the nineteenth century had persisted through the postwar boom, but were now being transformed into an *intra*-sectoral division of labour, the latter involving specialisation in different stages of the process of accumulation within the same industrial sector. Indeed, 'the geographical reorganisation of British capital within Britain. . . was an important element in its early response to impending crisis' (Massey 1986:37).

The process of national de-industrialisation made itself felt on this already changing geographical pattern, and it is possible to see three stages of regional decline in the reaction to the crisis at the national and international level. The first of these involved the major conurbations and saw the rise of the inner city problem at the end of the 1960s. During the 1970s, job loss in the traditional development areas showed similarities to the structural decline of the inter-war years, but was combined with a continuing process of decentralisation. The third stage involved the core British manufacturing belt from the late 1970s onwards. Let us look at these stages in more detail.

The first stage of regional decline, then, involved the collapse of the manufacturing base of large cities, and the inner city in particular, in prosperous and assisted areas alike. Fothergill and Gudgin (1982) saw this as a function of 'urban decline and rural resurgence', with the change in manufacturing employment in urban areas due to a differential shift, a function of residual factors which cannot be simply attributed to trends in the national economy. For them, this differential shift represented a massive flight of manufacturing employment and investment from the urban conurbations, towards the rural areas, with the fastest growing industries of the post-war boom leading the flight. Other commentators, however, place these changes in a wider perspective, and argue that these local variations 'were not fully autonomous of national and international structural forces' (Marshall 1987:200). Or as Dunford and Perrons (1986:90) put it 'the problem was mainly one of a restructuring and rationalisation of production aimed at increasing the rate of profit in a context of low investment and low output growth.'

From the beginning of the 1970s, two contradictory processes were at work in the development areas: rationalisation involving job loss on the one hand, and a continuing decentralisation with the creation of employment on the other. Both these processes were part and parcel of the national restructuring of capital associated with a shift in the strategy of capital towards neo-Fordism. Whilst the 1960s had seen some restructuring of existing capacity in the North East, notably in chemicals, the 1970s saw further disinvestment in oil and chemical production and in mechanical engineering. Yet like other regions, the North East was attractive for branches of production with a high and rising organic and technical composition of capital, thanks on the one hand to labour reserves, and on the other to central government financial incentives. The North East thus became a link in the global chain of corporate production and restructuring remarked upon in earlier sections. Already by 1971, 40 per cent of all manufacturing plants in the North East were either branch or subsidiary plants, while numbers employed in foreign-owned branch manufacturing plants rose from 8,500 in 1963 to 24,400 in 1971 and 45,000 by 1978 (Hudson 1986).

During the 1970s, then, the quantitative decline of manufacturing employment already commented upon at a national level, was accompanied by qualitative changes in ownership and control and technical organisation involving a spatial redistribution of such employment. These spatial consequences were seen in terms of 'external control' of regional development and exemplified in the 'branch plant economy'. However, 'it is not the control of development from external spatial sources which is so significant as the expanded strategic options over which that managerial control can be exercised' (Marshall 1987: 211). The problem is that the gains from inward investment may be short-lived, with further difficulties in subsequent rounds of corporate restructuring. An obvious example is the textile and garment industry. The later 1970s thus saw further cutbacks in employment, even in areas – such as the North East – where employment had been expanded during the early restructuring phase.

By the end of the 1970s, spatial inequalities were not merely visible in terms of the *quantity* of job opportunities, but also in the *quality* of working conditions and in the kind of jobs available. Job losses in the old industrial areas had lead to a decline of employment opportunities for traditionally-skilled, unionised, male manual labour, whilst new areas provided growth in employment opportunities for unskilled, poorly unionised female labour. Many other commentators would agree with Marshall that 'the process of industrial restructuring has involved a process of social recomposition or class restructuring' (Marshall 1987: 218). The restructuring process that went along with the establishment of branch plants in the North East, as in other British regions, was based on intra-sectoral spatial distinctions, as already mentioned. The result, as Massey (1979) suggests, is a three-fold spatial division of labour.

Mass production or assembly lines are located in areas of semi-skilled, low-waged, relatively poorly organised labour. This tends to be in areas, such as the North East, dominated by declining industries like mining, and with a formerly non-employed female population. Such branch plants have low internal linkages compared with the heavy industrial complexes which preceded them. At the second stage of accumulation, processes are not significantly automated, and involve skilled labour in the old nineteenth century cities. This stage is less significant now, its importance having been undermined during the first stage of regional decline at the end of the 1960s. The third stage of accumulation involves the concentration of higher management, research and development, and financial and professional service centres at the central metropoles. The growth of the microelectronics industry represents a typical example of the new spatial division of labour, with 'Silicon Glen' dominated by multinational branch plants and the final assembly process, whilst the M4 corridor focuses on research and development and specialised components and equipment. It is worth realising that the North East loss of jobs in electronics between 1971 and

1984 was, at 23,000, equivalent to those lost in the 'sunset' industries (Williams and Charles 1986). Thus although some regional convergence was being experienced during the 1970s, a gap was also growing between centres of management control located at the core, and areas with externally controlled industrial development, such as the North East, at the periphery.

Whilst the restructuring of the 1970s meant diversification in the range of industries in the regions, there was homogenisation of the labour process and types of work, and disparities in the types of employment opportunities available in the regions are probably as important as levels of employment in the longer run. Rhodes (1986), unfortunately looking only at the male workforce, shows that manual employees are more concentrated in the assisted and central regions, whilst non-manual employees are more concentrated in the southern regions. Over the period between the censuses of 1971 and 1981, the total labour force fell by 1 per cent, but manual employment fell by 7 per cent, whilst non-manual rose by 9 per cent. The regional picture shows that occupational disparities between the north and south of Britain have been widening rapidly over the decade. As Rhodes points out, the fact that the already existent bias of the North to manual labour is increasing, does much to explain disparities in unemployment rates between northern and southern regions, since manual, and particularly unskilled, workers have higher unemployment rates than non-manual.

This leads us to the third stage of regional decline in the reaction to the crisis at the national and international level. By the end of the 1970s the fragility of the restructuring process that had gone on earlier became apparent, as unemployment rates rose, particularly in the regions. The broadened options available to multinational companies who had set up branch plants at the periphery expressed themselves in a renewed round of restructuring. At this stage the structural adjustment to de-industrialisation involved national capitals abandoning domestic production altogether. A new phase of widening regional inequalities was beginning, made particularly clear by the creation of a new depressed region, that of the West Midlands. Decline had spread to areas which had led the economic growth process after the Second World War. The centre has thus shrunk relative to the periphery, and both old and new industrial sectors have been affected.

In the North East, as elsewhere at the periphery, disinvestment by private capital was a result of the area's decline in attractiveness for manufacturing capital. This was due on the one hand to the British state's macro-policy, and the regional effects of exchange rate policies and the abolition of control on capital movements; and on the other to the selective industrialisation of parts of Mediterranean Europe and the Third World (Hudson 1986). External control of regional development by multinational companies had probably hastened the collapse of smaller, indigenous firms, thus adding to the instability introduced into the local industrial and employment base. The election of the Thatcher government in 1979 also marked an important watershed in policy towards the nationalised industries, and as we have already seen, employment in the North East has been particularly reliant on state capital to provide jobs. The Thatcher government's policies of more restrictive monetary policies, cutting back on public expenditure, encouraging privatisation and limiting the power of trade unions have all meant pressures on nationalised industries to contract. The combined effect of public and private sector contraction is visible in the redundancy figures for the North East, and reflected in higher regional unemployment.

On Wearside it is very clear that a process of social, or class, and gender recomposition of the labour force has gone on alongside a process of economic restructuring. Setting the scene 2 showed how this happens at a personal level. Amongst the men, Mr Bolam and Mr Carrick were made redundant by plant closures, while Mr O'Brien and Mr Hogg were both affected by the long-drawn-out decline of the Sunderland shipbuilding industry, well prior to the Christmas 1988 Government announcement of its complete closure. In contrast with their husbands' experiences, the case studies showed wives finding and keeping low paid, 'women's jobs', often on a part-time basis: Mrs Carrick as a home help, Mrs Hogg as a school dinner lady. Very few were better paid, but Mrs Bolam had a position as a cleaning supervisor, and Mrs O'Brien was the exception in holding on to an operator's position in manufacturing, where jobs for women had once been plentiful during the early 1970s.

I will draw on the work of Stone and Stevens (1985, 1985–6) to analyse the changes that have taken place in the Wearside labour market since 1970, first looking at overall trends in labour demand and unemployment levels, and then at some of the changes in the structure of employment. It is worth pointing out that Wearside consists of two major centres of population with contrasting economic characteristics: there is the old industrial town of Sunderland based on shipbuilding and mining with its heyday at the beginning of the century on the one hand, and the new town of Washington with a range of new industrial plant on the other. Changing employment patterns in the two centres therefore tend to offset one another.

Table 2.1 shows that total employment on Wearside fell by 10 per cent in the period 1971 to 1981, a decline which was considerably greater than that for Britain as a whole, or for the northern region. Most of this decline was concentrated in the years between 1978 and 1981, as the recession deepened; but throughout the decade the growth of employment in Washington disguised a dramatic decline on the rest of

Wearside amounting to the loss of 17 per cent of jobs between 1971 and 1981. In the period between 1981 and 1984, the table shows that total employment on Wearside fell by a further 4.1 per cent, a greater fall than that for Britain as a whole, but a slightly better performance than that of the northern region, due largely to continued growth in the New Town. These changes in overall levels of employment, however, mask very considerable changes in the relative numbers of male and female workers on Wearside over the period. Whilst male employment declined by as much as 21 per cent between 1971 and 1981 (see Table 2.2), female employment actually rose by 9 per cent, a figure which admittedly included a period of relatively slow decline during the height of the recession between 1978 and 1981. Male job contraction occurs at a greater rate than that for either the country as a whole, or for the northern region.

Table 2.1 Comparisons of change in total employment on Wearside 1971–84

	Total employment			
	1971	1978	1981	1984
Wearside TTWA*	122,193	121,385	110,010	105,515
Northern Region	1,206,280	1,240,508	1,113,902	1,024,902
Great Britain	21,637,883	22,226,343	21,092,016	20,477,061
	Change in employment %			
	1971–78	1978–81	1971–81	1981–84
Wearside TTWA	-0.7	-9.4	-10.0	-4.1
Northern Region	2.8	-10.2	-7.7	-7.9
Great Britain	2.7	-5.1	-2.5	-2.9

*Travel to Work Area
Source: Stone and Stevens 1985

Women's employment rose faster than the rate for the region, but slightly slower than the national rate. Back in 1951, women accounted for only 29 per cent of total employment compared with 31 per cent nationally, and whilst women had comprised less than a third of the Wearside workforce in 1966, by 1981 they made up nearly 45 per cent. This was well above both the regional proportion of 42 per cent and the national proportion of 43 per cent. Between 1981 and 1984 there was a continuation of the trend away from male and towards female employment, such that by 1984 women made up 47.5 per cent of the Wearside workforce compared with 44.5 per cent regionally and 43.9 per cent in the country as a whole. Indeed, in Washington, women outnumber men in the workforce, and make up 51.3 per cent of the total.

Table 2.2 Comparative changes in male and female employment 1971–84

Men				
	1971–8	1978–81	1971–81	1981–84
Wearside TTWA	-8.0	-14.1	-21.0	-9.3
Northern Region	-2.8	-13.1	-15.6	-12.2
Great Britain	-2.5	-7.4	-9.8	-5.2
Women				
Wearside TTWA	12.0	-2.6	9.1	2.4
Northern Region	12.9	-5.8	6.3	-1.7
Great Britain	11.3	-1.8	9.3	0.2

Source: Stone and Stevens 1985

There are also marked changes in the proportion of part-time employment over the period, which particularly affected female employment, since part-time employment of men is relatively unimportant, being less common on Wearside than in other parts of the country. Whilst in 1971 the proportion of women working part-time on Wearside (33.3 per cent) was slightly lower than that nationally (33.5 per cent), by 1981 it had risen to 45.1 per cent above both the regional (42.7 per cent) and the national proportion (41.5 per cent). This trend also continued in the period up to 1984, with a 12.4 per cent increase in the number of female part-timers since 1981, so that by 1984 over 49 per cent of Wearside women were working part-time. As will be shown when examining the changing structure of employment on Wearside, most of this dynamism in part-time female job opportunities can be put down to the development of light manufacturing and service employment in the early and mid 1970s.

Unemployment rates on Wearside have remained at almost twice the national average since 1971, and also well above the rates for the northern region. Regionally, as nationally, men have always made up a large proportion of the unemployment figure, which can be explained in terms of the social security system and the 'discouraged worker'. Changes in the definition of unemployment by the present government have also meant that the increases in unemployment have been less than they would otherwise have been. The age distribution of unemployed men has become more concentrated in the 20 to 59 age group since 1971; reflecting legislative changes and the trend towards early retirement. The age distribution of unemployed women differs from the male pattern, for whilst there has been a decline in the proportion of under 20s and an increase in the over 25s, there has not been a decline in the oldest age groups, again particularly reflecting the impact of the social security system. The length of time that people remain out of work has also risen steeply over the period since 1971, in particular the rate of long-term unemployment. Long-term unemployment is higher than both the regional and national figures: in 1974, 36.7 per cent of men and 14.3 per cent of women on Wearside had been out of work for more than a year; by 1985 this had risen to 56 per cent of men and 38.2 per cent of women. The proportion of men and women out of work for more than a year had risen even more steeply, and by 1985 well over one third of unemployed men had been unemployed for over two years.

Changes in the pattern of employment and unemployment have thus been more marked on Wearside than either regionally, or especially nationally. In addition there have also been major changes in the structure of employment on Wearside since the beginning of the 1970s, such that 'the commonly held view of Sunderland – as a town characterised by heavy industry and with a male-dominated employment structure – needs to be revised' (Stone and Stevens 1985:ix). Taking the primary sector (mining, quarrying, and agriculture) first of all; this has traditionally provided a major source of employment for men on Wearside, essentially in coal mining. In 1971 coal still accounted for nearly 15 per cent of total employment, despite the substantial decline in mining jobs that had already occurred. Even after the decline of 43 per cent that occurred in the decade to 1981, the primary sector remains twice as important in the northern region as a source of employment, and three times as important as nationally. Employment in this sector is overwhelmingly in the public sector, and of course is almost all male.

In contrast, despite the traditional picture of Wearside as a centre of manufacturing, particularly in terms of shipbuilding and engineering, the proportion of the workforce employed in manufacturing has remained consistently below regional and national levels. In 1971, nearly 36 per cent of the Wearside workforce was employed in manufacturing, but by 1981 this proportion had declined to 27 per cent with nearly one third of all employment in this sector disappearing. Rates of decline of manufacturing employment were higher (at -32.9 per cent) than either regionally (-26.4 per cent) or nationally (-24.3 per cent).

Stone and Stevens (1985) estimate that rates of decline of manufacturing from 1981 to 1984 continued to be above the national average, but somewhat below that for the region. Whilst manufacturing on Wearside has always employed more male than female labour, the decline in female employment has been far steeper than that for men: a fall of 43 per cent as against 28.7 per cent. Thus the proportion of the growing female workforce employed in manufacturing fell from 29 per cent in 1971 to only 15 per cent in 1981. The period also saw a significant move towards part-time employment in manufacturing, particularly of course for women. The public sector makes up some 30 per cent of manufacturing, where almost all of the employees are men.

Looking in a little more detail at the process of restructuring and contraction in the manufacturing sector, there were falls in employment in all but five of the seventeen industrial orders making up the sector. The fall in employment was especially dramatic in the engineering and allied industries sector, which besides being the most important manufacturing employer on Wearside, declined at almost twice the national rate over the period 1971 to 1981. It is also noticeable that employment decline has been concentrated amongst large employers, on the one hand due to the contraction of traditional manufacturing activities especially in shipbuilding and engineering, and on the other to closures and cutbacks in branch plants attracted to the area in the post-war period. Stone and Stevens (1985) see manufacturing employment loss associated with three main processes, all of which reflect the impact of de-industrialisation on the local economy. The most significant cause of job loss is rationalisation and capacity reduction by branch plants, though there is also some intensification of production by local firms. The impact of the introduction of new technology on job loss up to the beginning of the 1980s was relatively small.

Looking finally at the service sector, this sector has experienced a more rapid growth rate than nationally, but from a lower base. In common with the national picture, services rose in importance in the Wearside economy, making up only 42 per cent of employment in 1971, but rising to 58 per cent by 1981, while between 1981 and 1984 it rose by a further 4.1 per cent compared with 1.9 per cent nationally and -0.6 per cent in the northern region. The service sector is of course dominated by female and part-time employment. In 1981, women made up two out of every three service sector jobs, and indeed 82 per cent of employed women worked in the service sector, while only 38 per cent of men did so. Over a third of service sector jobs were part-time, while for women alone half were part-time. Over 40 per cent of service jobs are in the pubic sector, a sector which is a more significant provider of jobs for men than for women.

Unemployed men and housework

Mr and Mrs Coulthard: a traditional rigid gender division

Mrs Coulthard works 4 hours a week on a regular baby-sitting job, whilst her husband lost his post in a local authority garage a year ago. The couple are both in their 50s. Out of six major regular household tasks (making the main meal, hoovering, washing, ironing, doing the household shopping, and washing-up), Mr Coulthard only sometimes helps with the washing-up. 'It gets a bit few and far between' as he puts it. He does however do all the decorating (a major occasional task), apart from his sons' rooms: they do their own. Of the many minor tasks, he shares making breakfast and sometimes makes snacks. Although he shares bed-making, he sees it as too minor to be a task. With some implications of a patriarchal attitude, he says of shopping for big items: 'we'd talk it over' (before his wife goes out to buy it). The contrast between their free time is striking: 'I've got loads of free time; too much really', so that in good weather Mr Coulthard will be under the car or out for a walk, 'something to fill the time', he says of his wife: 'I don't think she's got much free time, looking after me and the two lads'.

It is noticeable that the two sons (aged 24 and 18, and both in work) contribute to considerably more household tasks than their father. Mr Coulthard does, however, share looking after his 18-month-old grand-daughter with his wife on a regular basis. 'Its a second home to her – she knows where the biscuits are. I could keep her', he says with feeling. The childcare role is probably the only factor which might militate against the traditional rigid categorisation, but Mr Coulthard does point out that his daughter trusts him to look after the toddler only 'as long as she's already bathed'. His views on roles are highly traditional. He has a low view of housework and did not like his job in the garage since it involved cleaning. What he likes least about being unemployed is that 'it takes you out of the manly role. I used to be the breadwinner with my meal on the table. It lowers you. I feel like a lodger in my own house.'

Mr and Mrs Hogg: a traditional flexible household

We have already met the Hoggs: Mrs Hogg works 7¹/₂ hours a week as a school dinner lady, while her husband stopped working 3 years ago. Both husband and wife are in their 60s, being the oldest couple in the sample. Of the six major regular tasks, two are shared (the hoovering and the shopping) while Mr Hogg, does the washing-up. Indeed, according to Mrs Hogg, 'I don't do any now – I hate washing-up'. Mrs Hogg, however, does the four skilled major tasks: making the main meal, washing, ironing, and decorating. Her husband shares a fair number of the minor non-gender segregated tasks, though it is worth realising that all the shared tasks in this household are shared three ways with their 35-year-old son. In terms of the other sample families, this only son is singularly helpful. In other words, Mr Hogg's contribution is not as great as it might appear. 'On a Sunday', says Mr Hogg, 'we all have our little jobs. We just muck in on a Sunday'. Husband and son 'did everything' according to Mrs Hogg, when she was off sick with a bad back for three weeks recently, yet she says of her husband's vacuuming, 'he tickles round'.

Although the husband and wife share the responsibility for money, this has a patriarchal flavour. 'I've never seen his wage packet, but I've never gone without', declares Mrs Hogg. Both of them have fairly flexible attitudes to roles, perhaps partly because Mrs Hogg is planning to give up her job shortly and join her husband in retirement. 'We are getting on and we want to go places together.' Mr Hogg does housework, 'to save her doing it and to see the house tidy'. It seems in line with a traditional flexible form of organisation that this interview kept wandering off the point; although Mrs Hogg volunteered that she enjoyed the interview, neither of them had much invested in the issue of who should undertake housework.

Mr and Mrs Kidd: a sharing family

Mrs Kidd (aged 41) works twenty hours as a school cleaner, doing a split shift: early morning and late afternoon, while her husband (aged 46) was a sorter in the Post Office until 2 years ago. They have five children altogether: a son and daughter of secondary school age still live at home, together with a foster son. Mr Kidd shares three major tasks (making the main meal, hoovering, and shopping), and does two on his own (decorating and ironing). He is the only man to do all the ironing in the sample. 'I do that', he declares, 'she doesn't like it'. He also shares a number of minor tasks. On the other hand, Mrs Kidd undertakes the three responsibility tasks of planning meals, checking what is needed in the way of shopping and looking after the money.

Since Mrs Kidd only works 20 hours, this family is unlikely to be involved in exchanging roles, and indeed sharing is confirmed by her description of a typical day.

> I go out to work at 8.00 a.m. and have a bacon sandwich [Mr Kidd has made it] when I get in. Then we tidy up, with a few cups of tea in between and then have dinner. We put the washing in. He washes up and I prepare the tea [i.e. the main meal]. He makes me a cup of tea before I go out to work. He puts the tea on, we have tea at six, and he washes up.

Household tasks are very much shared in this picture, and they both see overall responsibility as shared between them.

For this family, sharing household tasks is important but natural. Mr Kidd says of men doing housework: 'It's a good thing now. Times have changed; it was always women's work. They should both share.' Asked whether they've discussed who does what, Mrs Kidd replies with some mirth, 'No. We just automatically do it don't we?' It is perhaps because sharing attitudes run quite deep in this family that Mrs Kidd does not mention 'bottoming'. ('Bottoming' is an exclusively female gendered activity mentioned at some time in the interview by over a third of the families; it is a local term which means pulling the furniture out and giving a thorough vacuum.) She does nevertheless seem to be the force behind the excellent job they are doing as foster parents.

Mr and Mrs Turner: an exchanged-role family

The Turners have four children altogether, of whom a son of secondary school age and a daughter in full-time work still live at home, together with a foster son of 13. Mrs Turner works full-time as a nursery nurse, while her husband worked as a sales person until 11 months ago. Both are in their mid 40s. The Turners are a typical example of an exchanged-role family. Of the major tasks, Mr Turner shares two, shopping and hoovering, though he always does the hoovering through the week. He also does all the decorating and has panelled the whole house out. 'I enjoy seeing what I've done.' Mrs Turner does the washing and ironing, but for the main meal, 'If I was tired, he would do it.' Their 14 year old daughter does the washing up; an example of the helpfulness of children in exchanged-role households. Mr Turner either does, or shares, a substantial number of minor tasks, and for instance, is unusual amongst husbands in undertaking to sweep and wash floors. His description of his typical day clearly indicates a domestic routine.

> I made the breakfast, took her to work, did the hoovering, washed the floor downstairs, and changed the furniture round. Then I

made their [the children's] dinners and did some more hoovering. By that time it was time to fetch my wife from work.

As Mrs Turner puts it: 'I've handed over all general housework, all of it. Now that he's not at work I do a quarter of the work that I used to do.' On the other hand, she still does some extra work at the weekend. 'I would do more washing and ironing at the weekend. More housework – what my husband wouldn't notice.'

They have never really discussed who should do what in the house, but according to Mrs Turner, 'I usually say, "Oh I must do this" and before I get a chance to do it, Arthur, if humanly possible, will do it.' Mrs Turner, as a full time nursery nurse, is now the breadwinner. 'Dole money just pays the rent', points out her husband. Mr Turner contributes to her paid work by taking and fetching her each day to Gateshead. Mrs Turner appreciates this, and other aspects of her husband taking on a domestic role: 'Taking me to work, bringing me back – that's luxury. So is coming in and having a cup of tea made.' There is, then, a considerable loosening of gender stereotypes in this family, and they have joint responsibility for money. Yet when asked what he feels in general about mothers working, Mr Turner replied, 'I wouldn't want her to work until it's necessary. You know I've always believed it's a man's place to work. I think married women shouldn't work.' There are vestiges, both of a traditional view of roles as well as traditional practice (weekend housework for women) even in exchanged-role families.

Chapter 3

Models of relevance to household work strategies

Models of the household

The structural economic changes examined in the last chapter have potential implications for gender divisions of labour inside and outside the household, and the concern of this chapter is to provide a framework from models which are of relevance to examining changing household work strategies. Setting the scene 3 has just given examples of the four different ways in which Wearside families experiencing male unemployment organise work within the household, and Part II will take the empirical analysis of such case study material much further. Having provided the reader with a flavour of the various domestic responses to having a husband at home while the wife is out at work, it is important to be aware of the theoretical framework within which empirical study can be placed. Though a wide variety of models are relevant to such a project, a broad distinction can be drawn between models primarily located in the household, and labour market theories.

Most important among the former are, on the one hand theories of the household in economic literature, primarily concerned with its consumption role; and on the other, the domestic labour debate and the labour process perspective, both of which focus on the productive role of the household. Labour market models of employment and unemployment tend to concentrate on the role of the male breadwinner, but over the last few years the focus has shifted to a perspective that is more relevant to the female experience. Thus recent models undertake to articulate these two broad strands by integrating labour market and domestic roles for women, initially through consideration of the life cycle. The evidence presented in Chapter 2 – employment records broken by unemployment and chequered job histories – indicates that men may need to adapt to their wives' work opportunities, and thus, indirectly, to domestic work requirements. It is important to ask whether men can be included within gendered models of the household and the labour market.

Finally, the concern to articulate the connections between work and home has taken place within a broader theoretical framework of feminism and patriarchy, where the role of ideology has played a considerable part. The chapter concludes with a consideration of two major areas where ideology is of considerable significance. First, the division of income within the household in terms of spending is an aspect of how power within the family is divided, and interesting links can be drawn between gender patterns of spending and incentives to participate in paid work. Given that the 'family wage' is unequally shared within the household, the very concept of the family wage can be questioned. Second, the state benefit system and the state's structuring of low pay do much to confirm traditional roles, and rely on the idea of a family wage earned by a male breadwinner.

Traditionally, and particularly for economists, the household unit has been regarded as a 'black box'. The household is one of the basic units of orthodox economics, forming a nexus which links the activities of consumption, of production, and of distribution; yet the ways in which these activities are undertaken within the household unit have been subsumed beneath assumptions that the household could be regarded as an individual.

Gary Becker was amongst the first of the orthodox economists to consider the household in more detail with a theory of the allocation of time (Becker 1965). He argued that by including time in a revised theory of choice he was able to integrate production and consumption. This involved the concept of 'full income' which he defined as the income that could be obtained by devoting all the time and other resources of the household to earning income, with no regard to time spent on consumption activities. This provides a meaningful resource constraint, and one based firmly on the fact that goods and time can be combined into a single overall constraint because time can be converted into goods through money income. The analysis thus treats all commodities symmetrically and stresses only their differences in relative time and earning intensities. Since, for example, the unemployed and women have lower foregone costs, they also have lower relative prices of time. In a process of circular reasoning, the division of labour in families rests on the fact that those members who are relatively more efficient at market activities will use less of their time on consumption activities.

Whilst Becker takes an important step forward in recognising the production activities of families, he can be criticised on two fronts. First, that he does not deal with gender issues or with power and authority within the family, and also that – as Himmelweit and Mohun (1977) point out – he fails to penetrate the actual relations of production involved; considering only products, and these products only as providers of utility. Scarcity as the only constraint on the freedom to choose is in any case inadequate: the economists' indifference curve assumes that people do what they want to do, and gives little attention to power and conflict within the family.

J. K. Galbraith launches a resounding attack on the mismatch between consumption and the orthodox concept of the household in *Economics and the Public Purpose* (1975) which is very much in the tradition of the early Institutionalist Economists. Expressing himself in a more accessible fashion than Becker, he argues that whilst consumption is conventionally seen as trouble-free enjoyment, rising standards of popular consumption and the disappearance of personal servants creates an urgent need for consumption to be managed. But unlike Becker, Galbraith is acutely aware of the gender implications of these developments, arguing that women have been converted into a crypto-servant class whose role is critical for the expansion of consumption in the modern economy. The household thus becomes a disguise for the role of women. 'Neo-classical economics resolves the problem by burying the subordination of the individual within the household, the inner relationships of which it ignores, Then it recreates the household as the individual consumer' (Galbraith, 1975:51).

This first strand in the literature which takes a closer look at the household is useful in highlighting that consumption activities involve work, and Vanek may well be correct in saying that 'a large amount of time devoted to homemaking probably reflects a family's tastes and its preference for a particular quality of life' (Vanek 1974:90). Yet such a statement raises the importance of both a non-individualistic, and a non-material theory of human needs, neither of which is tackled by Becker and those within the orthodox economic tradition. Chapter 5 will be looking at empirical evidence which points to the importance of these aspects, together with its significance for economic constructs. Further, as Andrew Tolson points out: 'the "consumer society" brought to final fruition a long-term tendency of industrial capitalism to divide "work" and "home", and to create a proletariat for which "leisure" home-centred family relationships is the reward for alienated labour' (Tolson 1977: 15). But ideas of affluence and leisure and a split between work and home are peculiarly masculine concepts, for there is no such split for the housewife. As Tolson concludes: 'definitions of gender enter into some of the basic meanings attached to work, leisure, family life' (ibid.:17).

One of the major advantages of the domestic labour debate, the theoretical strand to which I now turn, is that it is concerned with the productive aspect of women's role in the family and that it makes an important analogy between domestic labour and paid work. It is, how-ever, important to be aware that this debate, which took place in the mid 1970s, was an almost exclusively theoretical one, concerned with how domestic labour fits in with Marx's model. Indeed, the lack of concern for empirical aspects is highlighted by the use of the term 'domestic labour' instead of housework, and I shall argue in a moment that it is not easy to see how the theoretical concepts used in the debate could be empirically operationalised.

Controversy in the domestic labour debate focused on the relationship between domestic labour and wage labour in general. The concern was therefore with the significance of domestic labour for the capitalist mode of production. I do not propose to enter into details of the debate since there have already been several attempts at overviews of what went on. Close and Collins (1985) provide one of the most useful of these, and argue that there are four approaches involved in the debate. The first approach sees Marx's labour theory of value as valid and argues that domestic labour produces surplus value either by allowing workers to be paid below the value of their labour power, or by depressing the value of labour power through a cheapening of commodities. The second approach argues that the labour theory of value is inadequate; whilst the third sees the labour theory of value as valid, but that properly applied, it shows that domestic labour has no direct relation with capital. Finally, and this is the approach of Christine Delphy (1984), domestic labour should be seen as a separate mode of production.

Summarising on the most useful aspects of the debate, capitalism is seen as splitting the labour process into two discrete units; capitalist production on the one hand, and reproduction for capital on the other. The latter comprises domestic labour and involves both daily and generational care. A major concern here is that the commodities bought by the wage are not in consumable form, and that housework is necessary to convert them into regenerated labour power. This gender division of labour ensures different experiences of the family's relation to capital: 'for the husband this is a value-relation – his labour-power has only a use-value aspect, since the wage is transformed into use-values with which her labour maintains and reproduces her family' (Himmelweit and Mohun, 1977:29). What is also made clear by the domestic labour debate is that 'the overall standard of living of workers is not determined just by the wage bargain between labour and capital, as it appears to be in Marx's analysis, but also by the contribution of domestic labour' (Gardiner 1975:53). The wage bargain is thus not just struck between labour and capital, but with domestic labour as well, and indeed with the state, for the social wage.

There are, however, quite a number of problems in the way that this debate was conducted. It has already been pointed out that much of it focused on the 'functions' of domestic labour for capitalism. Considerable emphasis was therefore placed on the relation between domestic labour and the value of labour power, and whether domestic labour produced surplus value or not. Thus Himmelweit and Mohun claim that 'the ultimate purpose of this production [domestic labour] is to provide labour-power for sale as a commodity to capital in order that surplus value be produced' (Himmelweit and Mohun 1977:28). There are considerable difficulties both in arguing that housework is performed on behalf of capitalism and that capitalism might need domestic labour. Such a functionalist approach is unjustified, and leads to a debate which at times threatens to come close to medieval arguments about the number of angels on a pinhead. Indeed Barrett and McIntosh question whether it is possible to theoretically specify a general relationship between domestic labour and the value of labour power. They suggest that looking at the historical determination of the value of labour power implies that it is historically given, rather than theoretically determined (Barrett and McIntosh 1980).

Part of the difficulty arises from the assumptions which Close and Collins (1985) point out run through the domestic labour debate. The first is that it is unnecessary to define the constituent activities of domestic labour, while the second is that the performance of domestic labour can be identified with the role of wife and mother. Himmelweit and Mohun (1977:18) indeed insist on a definition of domestic labour – 'the labour that directly maintains and reproduces labour power' – which identifies it as women's labour. There is surely a need to operationalise domestic labour before looking at its functions, something that will be tackled in Chapter 4, when the empirical work in this field is looked at.

Coulson *et al* do point to the need to see the relative autonomy of women's oppression from the central axis of capitalist exploitation. A material basis for this arises, they argue, from the fact that the concept of abstract labour does not apply to housework and hence its specific character (Coulson, Magas, and Wainwright, 1975). But there is a need to go further than this, and to tackle issues which are not covered in the domestic labour debate, which fails to look at the relations between men and women as exemplified in housework. The question should concern what comprises the empirical connections between the capitalist mode of production, and gender relationships which operate by way of the practice of domestic labour. It is relevant here to keep in mind what Judy Wajcman has to say about the misleading nature of the analogy between domestic and paid work, for what is crucial is that capitalism has separated the two.

The conditions under which the two different forms of labour [domestic and waged] are now performed are quite different. It is

71

on the basis of marriage and motherhood, not of the wage, that the
housewife's work is related to social labour.

(Wajcman 1983:11)

Finally, whilst some attempts are made to link women's domestic
work and women's labour market work, this is not really an issue that is
tackled in any detail in the domestic labour debate. Wally Seccombe
does raise it in his second article, but in a manner which does much to
emphasise the gulf between theory and empirical reality. Thus he is
surely being hopelessly optimistic when he says that 'if the additional
goods and services bought with a second wage could not significantly
reduce domestic labour time, then the alternative of taking an outside
job could never exist for married women' (Seccombe 1976:91). Alas,
the alternative exists all too often!

It seems to me that despite Close and Collins' hope that it should be
possible to link the activities subsumed under housework with the
theoretical debate, this is in reality a very difficult task. I feel that it
would actually be more fruitful to start from an empirical base which
analyses the labour process within the family sufficiently. As Heidi
Hartmann says: 'who benefits from women's labour? Surely capitalists,
but surely also men, who as husbands and fathers receive personalised
services at home' (Hartmann 1979:6). In Setting the scene at the start of
this chapter it was shown that four distinct responses to male unemployment were in evidence when wives continue to be employed. Mr
and Mrs Coulthard 'carry on in the old way', while Mr and Mrs Hogg's
domestic organisation shows similarities with that of some retired couples. The other two families have less gender differentiated patterns: Mr
and Mrs Kidd share many domestic tasks, while the Turners have
adopted the most gender congruent roles of all.

It is ironic that many of the individuals who theorised in the domestic
labour debate had also undertaken empirical investigations into the
labour process, albeit not the domestic labour process. Both were informed by Marxism, yet the labour process debate revived the practice
of seeing work, not just as an economic category, but as a relation
between human beings. Of course neither domestic nor waged work are
simply economic relations, but even when married women are employed there is still a financial basis for marriage as a relationship of
inequality. Yet in the domestic labour debate, the gender subordination
of women was often reduced to a by-product of class processes. As
Cynthia Cockburn points out, we need to speak, not only of a mode of
production, but of a sex/gender system (Cockburn 1983). An examination of the labour process within the family allows of this possibility,
and this will be the concern of Chapter 4.

Labour market models of employment and unemployment

Just as models of the household relate primarily to women, so those of the labour market relate primarily to men. I propose to restrict my examination of models of employment and unemployment to those which are of most relevance to women's employment experiences. Four can be identified, and in order of relevance, they are: the neo-classical, the dual labour market, and the reserve army models, and finally those models which articulate the labour market and domestic roles of women. Neo-classical models of the development of human capital have now largely been abandoned. Such models argue that women develop less human capital than men, due to their interrupted work histories. The problem with this approach is that the division of labour within marriage is taken as given.

This first model has been largely replaced by that of segmented labour markets, of which dual labour market theory is a variant. This latter argues that there are few points of access to the primary labour market, which is characterised by high levels of pay and of job security; and that subsequent access is restricted by both employers and trade unions. Women do not even share equally in access to initial points of entry, thanks to their lower levels of education and training, but especially on re-entry to the labour market, women tend to go to the secondary market which is both low-paid and has poor job security.

The dual labour market then, accounts not only for inequalities of pay, but for the segregation of women in particular industries, both of which were shown to be features of women's employment in Britain in the last chapter. In the primary sector, the best paid jobs are by up-grading, while the secondary sector has fewer promotion possibilities and many points of entry. In other words, interrupted work histories are a major source of women's segregation. Dual labour market theories are a substantial advance on neo-classical labour market theory and can be linked in with empirical studies on the life cycle and female re-entry into the labour force, such as Martin and Roberts' (1984) work. The theory nevertheless does not explain public sector employment very well, which – until the end of the 1970s – was characterised both by job security and by limited promotion prospects. It must be remembered of course that some professional women belong to primary labour markets (Wilson 1987).

The advantages of Marxist concepts of the reserve army of labour are that they contain a dynamic element, which both provides an explanation for the expansion of female employment during the 1970s, and which links types of unemployment to types of employment. Marx argues that capital needs an industrial reserve army as a lever for accumulation on two counts: as a population that can be brought in or ejected from the labour force as the market expands or contracts, and as a population that acts as a competitive force. No section of the working class is entirely dependent for its costs of reproduction upon wages because of state benefits. One can distinguish along two dimensions between, on the one hand, those sections who are predominantly dependent on the wage, and those who are not; and on the other, those sections dependent upon sources other than the state for costs of reproduction, such as women dependent on the family. It is then noticeable that the position of married women can be classified along both these dimensions as preferred sources for the industrial reserve army (Beechy 1977). Women have the advantage for capital of being equivalent to semi-proletarianised workers, so that whilst women can disappear into the family when discarded from production, men become dependent on the state. The concept of the reserve army, then, has an explicit political function, which links in with the 'marginalisation' of groups.

Whilst useful, there are still some gaps in reserve army theories. As Martin and Roberts (1984) point out, there is a need to take structural and institutional economic change into account, especially such changes in the structure of employment as were described in the pre- vious chapter. Thus increased female participation rates in the 1970s were partly explained by the changing structure of employment and the shift towards services. As already shown, the sharp decline in the manufacturing sector from 1979–81 affected men more, although the participation of women in manufacturing was also heavily hit during this period. The theory also omits the links with the family production role examined above in the last section. Indeed, the meaning of unemployment still derives from a meaning of work which is narrowly defined as a numerated, paid, full-time, and continuous activity which takes place outside the home (Evans 1984).

Since 1980, numerous studies have been published which have been concerned to examine the interrelations between women's domestic and labour market roles. They have all made use of the concept of the life cycle, first introduced by Beynon and Blackburn, which distinguishes five typical stages in a woman's life: that before marriage, the period of marriage before any children are born, the period when children are young, when children are older and making considerable demands on parental income, and finally when the mother is free of children and so free to work (Beynon and Blackburn 1972). There are two interesting aspects to these recent studies. The first is the asymmetry in the studies which relates to work-role characteristics and family life: it is assumed that men's work-role characteristics affect their family lives, but that women's family lives affect their work (Voydanoff 1987). Secondly, they all have a strong empirical basis, so that the theory of articulation arises directly from the empirical work itself. There have been two sorts of study: large scale, predominantly quantitative studies arising out of the Office of Population Census and Survey's (OPCS) work on women and employment; and a range of smaller, qualitative studies which have examined the interaction of home and work for women in a range of employment experiences.

Martin and Roberts, in their analysis of the OPCS survey on women and employment, argue that existing definitions of unemployment, relate to administrative statistics and male concepts of lifetime economic activity and may not be appropriate for women in the 1980s (see Martin and Roberts 1984:chapter 7). They propose a continuum between unemployed and permanently economically inactive as more appropriate, a continuum which requires knowledge of both a woman's present situation, and her future plans, in order to place her. Martin and Roberts thus distinguish five groups of 'non-working' women: the unemployed (waiting to take up a job, looking for work, or sick), others looking for work (not working for domestic reasons, but would take up a job, or are looking for one), those planning to work within the next year, those planning to work in a year or more, and those who will not or may not work again. They point out that these categories are fluid in terms of time, and that unemployment registration cuts across the categories to some extent. Martin and Roberts indicate that unemployment for women is conditioned by women undertaking unpaid work at home in addition to work in the labour market.

Cragg and Dawson (1984) extend this work by looking in more detail at the attitudes and experience of unemployed women. They point out that the majority of women in their sample did not regard themselves as 'unemployed'. The factors involved in this self-perception included that they were not seeking full-time work, that a proportion with children at home were not without work anyway, that some returners saw their status as arbitrary, that others associated unemployment only with severe financial constraints; nor did the majority of women see themselves as under any social pressure to work. Cragg and Dawson thus argue that unemployment is qualitatively different for women as opposed to men, and see women as having ambivalent attitudes towards work and home. The combination of work and housework is seen as a compromise rather than an ideal. As these authors see it, there is a stereotyped view that the division of labour in most households is governed by a simple domestic bargain, but they found that many of the women in their sample were discontented with their side of the bargain, so that in practice there was tension over it. Again, women's views of unemployment are conditioned by the double burden of work that those in the labour market bear.

When one examines the qualitative work in the field, it becomes apparent that, useful as the OPCS studies are in providing distinctive classifications for women, the relationship between home and work that they present is a somewhat mechanical one. Marilyn Porter, who looked at a small sample of working-class women, argues that when women enter the labour force, they do so as 'migrants from the domestic domain' (Porter 1982). The inadequacy of the family wage paid to their husbands meant there was pressure on them to earn money to make their task easier. Thus these women exemplify the integral connection between the spheres of production and reproduction:

> women at home are part of several interlocking spheres; that of production, consumption, and reproduction; that of the sexual division of labour organised around the family; and that of their own lives where they enter and leave the labour market at different points.

> (Ibid.:113)

Women thus see themselves in the labour market on quite different terms from men. Anna Pollert in her study of women working in a Bristol tobacco factory makes similar points; whilst these women rejected their place in the home, they felt they had no right to a job.

> The roots of this contradiction sprang from their dual identification as dependent wives in the family and as workers selling their labour power. Their oppression as women explained and defined their consciousness of exploitation as workers .

> (Pollert 1981:86)

Whilst it is true that both men and women discuss their families at work, it is on very different terms. Men discuss them as father and breadwinner, whilst for women it is the daily concern with the actual processes of family care that alters their consciousness of work. For women, 'work is overshadowed by the family' (ibid.:113).

The importance for women of the intermeshing of employment and domestic roles is taken further by Judy Wajcman (1983) and Frances Evans (1984). As the former points out, orthodox industrial sociology would find it hard to explain a working-class women's co-operative in the heart of the Norfolk countryside. Wajcman argues that this can be understood through a more clearly specified consideration of the life cycle, including not merely its economic, but also its psychological and ideological aspects. The life cycle certainly takes a cultural rather than a 'natural' form, with social expectations of appropriate behaviour at each stage. However,

> in order to explore the differences in orientations of women employees beyond those depending on whether they are single or

married with children, it is necessary to treat the household economy seriously, by examining the distribution of labour and resources within it over time. Otherwise it is unclear what the life cycle means for women apart from a general reference to responsibilities for childcare.

(Wajcman 1983:14)

This points to the importance of studying overall household work strategies.

This is not to say that the life cycle does not impinge on men too, whose experience of work is also mediated by the family, but for men this is primarily a financial strain. However, returning to women, it is not childcare constraints alone which impinge via the life cycle position on their commitment to work. Childcare is only part of what is understood to be women's work, and the sexual division of labour demands both engaging in paid work, and performing housework, especially given men's low wages. Thus although families are under financial strain when children are young, social convention precludes women going out to work until the fourth stage of the life cycle. The solution then is often to work part-time, whilst the full-time workers at Fakenham were all (with one exception) without heavy domestic commitments. So

working class (*sic*) women and men occupy sexually differentiated spheres and . . . this leads to diverging perceptions of work. Whereas men's identity and work roles are relatively integrated, for women work as a source of social identity is largely displaced by the domestic roles of wife and mother.

(Ibid.:49)

Frances Evans (1984) too, is concerned to demonstrate the importance of specificity when considering the interrelations between paid employment and domestic work. A woman's cycle of opportunities will be limited by both class and gender, and women's life experience can be seen in terms of changing roles and changing hierarchies of identity over the life cycle. To make sense of particular jobs, they need to be placed in a sequential context, which use of concepts of 'travel' and 'routes' allows. In retrospect, employment can be patterned in accordance with mobility – upward, downward, or immobile – and whether it is continuous or intermittent. Similarly, both the content of domestic labour, and attitudes to it, can change over the life cycle. Based on her empirical work, Evans notes the close links between women's attitudes to domestic labour, their domestic practices and their activity in the paid labour market. Ambiguity and confusion are the hallmarks of the demands made on women.

There is, then, a need to be cautious in the use of life cycle analysis to analyse women's employment experiences. As Stubbs and Wheelock (1989) point out in a study of women's employment potential on Wearside, women neither fit the stereotype of the conventional nuclear family household on the one hand, nor does their labour market behaviour fit into neat patterns on the other hand. We found many women with experiences of marital breakdown, or of single parenthood, and our study showed such women as likely to take their breadwinning role seriously, often not satisfied by the minimal levels of income available on benefit. There is also the very real contribution that women in a conventional nuclear household make to family income, or the 'family wage'. Interestingly, women themselves often define such a contribution as an 'extra', though including mortgage payments, debt repayments, or children's clothes.

As paid workers, Wearside women show a strong commitment both to the idea of paid employment in general, and a strong pride in their work. Few of those who were currently out of the labour market, whatever their domestic situation, were happy with the prospect of remaining out of a job for long. The costs for women of juggling paid employment with domestic responsibilities were well recognised by our respondents. The paradox was that although paid employment was seen by the vast majority as necessary for their own self-confidence and esteem, as well as for the material well-being of their families, it was also perceived as involving tensions, additional work, and often the guilt of not living up to the ideal of the 'good' wife, mother, or daughter.

In our study, Cherrie Stubbs and I concluded that although childcare is a major and pervasive factor affecting women's employment, it is by no means the only one, for in addition to care of older relatives, labour market factors also operate to affect women's employment chances. Most significantly, neither children's needs nor other domestic constraints operate in isolation. 'It is the way in which they connect to family relations, low pay, state benefits and availability of convenient jobs that is the issue' (ibid.). We found women who had been able to take full-time jobs with very young children and others with responsibilities to parents forced to leave the labour market even though they had no young children, and concluded that

> women fit neither into neatly phased employment patterns, nor domestically determined employment situations, whatever their circumstances. The main similarities of women as paid workers comes at another level, perhaps best encapsulated by the idea of 'flexibility', a characteristic much prized in the current economic climate.

(Ibid.)

It is this characteristic of 'flexibility' which can be used as a unifying concept when we consider in the next section, how men, as well as women might be included in models which take a wider view of work. This section has shown how a systematic consideration of women's labour process both within and outside the household provides a means of integrating gender models – which have primarily been adopted for women's work – and job models, which have been used for men. This is in contrast with, for example, adopting segmented labour market theories where women's oppression is seen as rooted in the labour market. It provides a strong theoretical basis for acknowledging the importance of overall household work strategies, which need to be examined in the context of the domestic labour process. The empirical work which is analysed in the second part of the book relies on just such a labour process approach.

Patriarchy, men, and gendered models

It has already been suggested on the basis of the evidence provided in Chapter 2, that there are now a number of ways in which men's labour market experiences are beginning to match women's, at least in terms of certain superficial indicators like broken employment patterns, long periods out of the labour market and chequered job histories. Given the analysis of the changing structure of male employment opportunities, and particularly of working-class males in the regions, it would not be surprising to find this growing similarity between women's and men's experiences. Indeed a number of relatively small-scale studies indicate just such an outcome. Lydia Morris, for example, suggests that although broken labour market experiences may be more common now, there is a long tradition of such patterns in Hartlepool, involving contract work in construction, in engineering, and in the oil and gas related construction boom (Morris 1987:90). The West Midlands Low Pay Unit similarly documents the growing importance of temporary work in the DHSS and in the Severn Trent Water Authority (Potter 1987).

At the same time Chapter 2 also made clear that there is a relative buoyancy in female work opportunities, again especially in the regions. Indeed, widespread unemployment amongst men makes the idea of the breadwinner an insult, and changes in the structure of employment undermine the traditional role of the man as the worker-earner and his wife as the housewife-carer. This twofold change in the gender structure of the labour market indicates that men may need to adapt to their wives' work opportunities, and so, indirectly to domestic work requirements. Indeed, in Setting the scene at the start of this chapter, the case studies of the Kidds, who have a sharing form of household organisation, and of the Turners, who exchange roles, indicate considerable variations from conventional gender stereotypes amongst husbands who are at home. In other words, the forces of structural economic change mean that it might be increasingly appropriate to fit men into gendered models. Additionally of course, substantial changes in family structure, particularly the growing importance of single parent families where women tend to be heads of household, mean that the traditional gender model is increasingly inappropriate. There may thus be a need to articulate both men's and women's domestic and labour market roles by extending a labour process perspective to *family* work strategies.

Many readers will no doubt see any idea that women's and men's employment experiences could be analysed within the same model as naive and optimistic. In particular it would appear to be ignoring the gender specific variables involved in women's work, deriving especially from the dual work role they perform. As I shall be indicating shortly, people's ideas and beliefs are a very powerful social force operating against the material forces of changing employment structure. So whilst changing employment patterns may be pushing towards less gender segregation of roles, patriarchal ideology – which can perhaps best be seen encapsulated in the concept of the family wage – restrains it. Nevertheless, it is important to pause to examine the similarities of experiences for women and men, and the core-periphery model of the restructured firm or industry with its emphasis on workforce flexibility is of especial relevance with regard to labour market links. It is also possible to connect men's and women's household work strategies by examining models of the negotiation process over the gender division of labour within and outside the household, where patriarchal ideology may be of particular importance.

Elements of the core-periphery model of the firm have already been mentioned as part of the neo-Fordist work strategies of employment in the last chapter. The growth of part-time employment and high turnover rates, particularly in relation to women have been highlighted. Neo-Fordism also involves a shift in the structure of industrial relations, changing the shape of traditional working patterns, and involving a serious threat to trade unions and to the quality as well as quantity of employment. Labour 'flexibility' is a term that is now very widely used and it has been seen as both an employers' and as a government tactic. The Conservative political argument that flexibility is essential to economic regeneration; and its concomitant policies of privatisation, labour mobility, paycutting, and the dismantling of protective legislation, have been given a particularly high profile.

The fundamental concern of the core-periphery model is with the segmentation of the internal labour market of the firm. Flexibility can be seen as having two elements: functional flexibility, where the existing workforce is used more efficiently; and numerical flexibility, where part-time, temporary, and subcontracted workers are used. The labour market within the firm divides between a core group of workers with functional flexibility making up the primary labour market, and a peripheral group with numerical flexibility making up a two-tier periphery. Many elements of flexible working have always been present within the workforce, but it is now being argued that the systematic use of a package of flexible working patterns has started to change the balance between a decreasing core and an expanding periphery, leading to a long-term shift in emphasis between the two.

As Meager (1986) suggests in a study of temporary work in Britain, three factors could have influenced the proportion of temporary workers in the employed workforce since the mid 1970s: the economic cycle, where temporary employment varies pro-cyclically; structural changes in employment, especially the growth of services relative to manufacturing; and new manning practices aimed at greater flexibility in employment. The evidence is that all three factors have been operating in the same direction to explain the growth in temporary work in recent years. However, Meager points out that in the Institute of Manpower Studies (IMS) sample used, larger and faster growing employers were more likely to use temporary workers, consistent with both cyclical and flexible manning (*sic*) influences. When the rationales for the use of temporary workers are examined, traditional rationales, such as cover for sickness, holidays, maternity leave etc., seasonal fluctuations, and covering shortages of permanent staff, still predominate.

However, new rationales – associated with being more flexible in the face of uncertainty and volatility in markets, and with avoiding the commitment to permanent staff – were given more often by employers who had increased their use of temporary workers since 1980, and were particularly apparent in the manufacturing sector. The study by the IMS then, tends to support the core-periphery model of the segmentation of the internal labour market of the firm. It is a pity that as yet there have not been any other major studies of this phenomenon, although it is widely seen as something that is going on extensively in the developed capitalist economies.

The peripheral labour market of the firm is often seen as a female ghetto, and of course it is true that flexibility was first noticed in relation to women. Women in employment are flexible in a number of ways. In the Wearside study already mentioned we found that this included that 'they are flexible in that a number of them are prepared to undertake work that is responsible, and involves a good deal of autonomy, but is rarely recognised as skilled' (Stubbs and Wheelock 1989:29). Women's willingness to undertake part-time or temporary work is a further aspect of their flexibility, and above all else, women are 'lifetime flexible' in that rarely does a female employee embark on a job for life, and few think in lifelong career terms. We, and others, conclude that 'women's "flexibility" in employment is fundamentally tied to the priority that domestic responsibilities still assume'. True, part-time and other flexible employment patterns fit the real needs of women and their families,

> but these needs are constructed from a lifetime in which women bear the brunt of negotiating a system in which neither male nor female wages are high enough to support the idea of a single family wage. . . . 'Flexibility' is one way in which women's dependency within such a system is reproduced.
>
> (Stubbs and Wheelock 1989:29)

It is of course true that women do predominate in part-time and temporary work, and for example, in the IMS sample mentioned above, 63.7 per cent of temporary workers were female, compared with less than 45 per cent of the total workforce. There remains a question however, as to how far the over-representation of women in the peripheral labour market is a 'demand side' and how far it is a 'supply side' phenomenon, and thus the extent to which peripheral status is likely to spread to male workers.

Recent articles by Joan Smith (1984) and Elizabeth Wilson (1987), relating to the American and British economies respectively, throw further light on this issue. Smith points out that demand side developments have been important, in that expansion of temporary and part-time employment has been linked with the dramatic growth in the service sector, where traditional 'women's occupations' are concentrated. These developments, however, are not just the unplanned outcome of typical employment practices, but are fundamentally tied to two conditions of operation in the service sector; namely the low capital to labour ratio, and the highly competitive nature of the business environment. Jobs offered in the service sector are nevertheless shaped by supply side presumptions that women have access to support beyond their own earnings. 'In short, the contemporary economy has moved to centre stage a labour force that must continually be endowed with marginal characteristics' (Smith 1984:300).

Whilst Smith is careful to point out that in the United States during the decade of the 1970s, almost twice as many part-time jobs went to women as opposed to men, she also draws attention to the fact that men and women increased their part-time work at almost the same rate. 'This strongly suggests that the growth in overall part-time labour, rather than rising from putative gender-based preferences, resulted from changes in the form and content of available work' (ibid.:305). In addition, she throws doubts on the idea that all women want part-time work: of the disproportionate increase during the 1970s in women's labour force participation rate, 73 per cent of women workers *not* with husbands took part-time work, whilst only 28 per cent of married women and 51 per cent of women overall took part-time work.

Wilson is also concerned to demonstrate, from a rather different perspective, that flexibility is not a policy that relates exclusively to women. In fact, she points out, the employment policies pursued by the Conservative government since 1979 have not affected all women equally, but have widened the gap between better-off and poorer women. For whilst there is some segmentation of labour markets for women, other women belong to the primary sector. Women's earnings no longer have the equalising effect that they used to on family earnings, because on the one hand, more jobs have been created for well-educated women, and on the other there has been a loss of women's jobs in manufacturing. 'Rather than making a specific attack on women as a homogeneous group, then, the present government has mounted a direct class attack' (Wilson 1987:207). She sees women being used to pave the way for a significant deterioration in the terms and conditions of employment, with the result that low wage policies have 'undergone a distortion such that they have borne particularly harshly on women, although less for ideological than for directly economic reasons' (ibid.: 210). Indeed, just as Smith emphasises, women can be drawn into the production process through deskilling and the disposal of male labour.

Whilst Smith and Wilson would agree then, that there is no necessary link between flexibility and the female workforce, and that this phenomenon extends to men too, they and others are concerned to point out that the new poverty created by this process is primarily a female impoverishment. It is the combination of structural economic change with changes in technology and consumption patterns together with changing family structures that has pauperised women and led to the 'feminisation of poverty'. The number of one parent families in the United States nearly doubled between 1970 and 1981, and in Britain they rose by two-thirds, yet 'those industries most responsible for employment growth pay a wage rate that absolutely requires the recipient of those wages to find additional resources in order to support a family above the poverty level' (Smith 1984:307). Basically, a gender bias in the restructuring process, combined with changes in family structure, has meant that women have been particularly affected by the process of economic change, but Smith and Wilson argue that men are also subject to the increasing reliance on flexibility.

No consideration of the ways in which men's work experiences might be replicating women's would be complete without a consideration of household work strategies, and the process of negotiation between the sexes over the division of labour both within and outside the household. The stereotyped view is that the division of labour in most households is governed by a simple domestic bargain where 'A corollary of the assumption that men were "supposed to" be the bread-winners was that women were "supposed to" do the housework' (Cragg and Dawson 1984:65). Any such process of negotiation involves four interrelated variables. First, there is the work itself, which is of two sorts: external and paid, or internal and unpaid. Then there is the income derived from work, or from other sources such as the state, where both who earns and who spends are important. Third, are the needs of the family; and finally there is the leisure, or non-work time, enjoyed.

Whilst this issue will be looked at empirically in the second part of the book, the concerns of this chapter are with models. Yeandle (1984) provides a useful theoretical framework for how negotiations can be resolved, distinguishing between negotiation on the basis of tradition, or patriarchy, and of rationality, with the maximisation of economic interests. She points out that the resolution reached between spouses will also depend on the stage of the life cycle and on broader economic circumstances such as high male unemployment and the changing structure of the labour market, but does not herself examine these aspects of the negotiating process. Chapters 4 and 5 will examine empirically how work strategies may vary with changes in economic circumstances, but let us now look in more detail at a negotiating framework.

Take the first variable: work. Negotiation depends crucially on the income obtained from it. It is immediately apparent that the household negotiating process is based on an imbalanced gender work situation. The domestic work – largely undertaken by women – is performed on the basis of motherhood and marriage, which as we have already seen, is in contrast with paid work done on the basis of the wage. Domestic work is seen and experienced as personal service, rather than as productive labour, and it is of course unpaid. Marriage thus has a different meaning for women and men, so that 'there is a conflict between a woman's responsibilities towards other members of her family and her activities in the labour market, whereas for most men there is not' (Land 1978:260). In order to combine unpaid domestic labour with wage labour, women have to adopt 'strategies for employment', of which Yeandle (1984) has identified three: household, family, and personal ones. Household strategies involve enlisting the help of other members of the household, mostly husbands and children, though it is impoitant to realise that this strategy is of limited use to single parent families. Family strategies involve kin, and here again of course, some women have no access to this strategy. Personal strategies can take three forms: reliance on commercial or *ad hoc* arrangements, working part-time or homeworking, and working very long hours. Yeandle sees part-time or homeworking as a useful partial solution to undertaking paid work and domestic labour. When the tasks of domestic labour fall overwhelmingly to women, this is an economically rational option for women to follow. But this in turn depends on women and men taking the traditional view of ideas and beliefs in gender roles as given.

Economic rationality must take account of employment opportunities, levels of pay, and access to state benefits for both husband and wife. It is the combination of employment opportunities for women, together with the low pay of men, which has encouraged married women in particular to undertake paid employment. Yet it remains the case that women's levels of pay are even lower than men's, and that wives have generally less entitlement to state benefits than their husbands. So whilst it may be economically rational for wives to undertake paid employment *as well* as their husbands, it is generally irrational for them to do it *instead* of their husbands. Nor is it economically rational for men to reverse roles, since their levels of pay tend to be higher than those of their wives.

This economic rationality is however strongly reinforced by ideological perceptions of the woman's wages as of secondary importance to her husband's. Three related ideological factors are at work here: that the man is seen as the breadwinner, that the woman is seen as the homemaker, and that wages are seen as payment for individual work (Hunt 1978). Their effect is particularly visible in patterns of spending within households. As we have already seen, the wife's income is perceived as purchasing extras, despite the fact that her income may be used for items such as mortgage payments, holidays, children's clothes, or savings. A wife's income is usually regarded by the family as a windfall, not as a basic source of supply, and this reinforces the ideology of the woman as a homemaker. In addition, as Hunt points out, 'the houseworker's claim to a share of the wage is on the whole made not as a co-worker, but as a member of the family consumption collective' (ibid.:561). The woman's attitude to money is thus related to her function, which is to make money stretch.

The concept of the family wage can thus be challenged because the wage is unequally shared within the household, and as has been variously pointed out by Land (1978), Morris (1987), and Pahl (1983) male spending-money is often a protected category. Wives thus have a double pressure on them to go out to work, at least on a part-time basis: on the one hand, women perceive a need for additional money for the household over and above the wages which their husbands can command, and on the other it provides the woman herself with a measure of financial self-sufficiency. Inequality in spending patterns within households provide an economic pressure for women to combine paid employment with their domestic tasks. 'Most men do not have this obligation, and that is one of the advantages that marriage has for most men' (Land

1978:283). Women's behaviour is thus subject to both the patriarchal view and to economic rationality. Within a traditional, patriarchal framework, it is economically rational for women to undertake two jobs.

Economic rationality thus means different things to different members of a family, since men and women have unequal access to the family wage. In addition, economic rationality is in any case over-determined by the ideology of patriarchy, and this is still further re-inforced by the role of the state in providing welfare. Thus the social security system ignores the fact that most families are dependent on two earners, actively discourages role-reversal, and encourages women to give priority to the home (Land 1978).

Perceptions of household needs are also part of the negotiating process over household work strategies. Again resolution may be on the basis of tradition or of rationality, but the relative importance of each will depend crucially on the stage of the life cycle. When children are young, tradition tends to predominate, when the financial strain is borne through a combination of men working long hours and their wives making ends meet. Needs are tailored to a single wage in many house-holds, and it is during these years when the wife is at home, that husbands get used to consuming rather than producing the comforts of the home. Once children are at school, rationality becomes relatively more important, since it is now socially acceptable for women to go out to work. Teenage children are particularly expensive to bring up, yet it is at this stage that manual workers are past their prime, and less able to earn extra income. Wives – due also to their subordinate position with respect to spending family income – are thus particularly subject to the economic pressures to supply the additional money needs of a growing family.

Finally, there will be negotiation over leisure-time within the family. Just as traditional ideology makes a substantial contribution to the contrast between men's and women's experiences of the family and work, reinforcing the economic constraints on the gender division of labour; so too does it contribute to contrasting experiences of leisure. Indeed gender inequalities in access to leisure are linked to differing gender perceptions of work. Paul Willis and Andrew Tolson examine this in relation to definitions of masculinity, though they also have a good deal to say about the stereotypes of femininity. As Willis points out, 'a central and defining feature of womanhood in our society is still a very definite set of expectations about her in relation to work' (in Clarke *et al.* 1979:186). Women are expected to do 'light' work, with low status and rewards, and to give it up for children, providing an 'emotional' home for the family and the 'breadwinner'. The wage packet is a prize for masculinity at work, a world which is too tough for the woman. The nature of masculine work thus becomes a style of teleology, while femininity is associated with a fixed state. 'Its labour power is considered as an ontological state of being, not a teleological state of becoming. Housework is not completion. It is rather a maintenance of status' (Clarke *et al.*:1979).

The male working identity carries over into the home in an idealised image of home-centred leisure, but which takes for granted an idealistic picture of the 'companionate' working-class family. 'Because the insistence on domestic "harmony" is, at root, a defence of male supremacy, the balance of a man's identity hangs upon the demarcation of domestic responsibilities' (Tolson 1977:70). It is small wonder that we find wives doing more domestic work, and having less leisure-time than their husbands at weekends, even if both are undertaking full-time paid work. Cynthia Cockburn also develops the links between work and masculinity in *Brothers* and comments on the irony of the man's situation in the house: 'A man's position at home is one of power. But that power is contingent on his absence all day at work' (Cockburn 1983: 134). Judith Chaney reckoned that an entrenched sexual division of labour is to be found amongst Sunderland's working class, fed from ideological roots: 'it appeared that the affirmation of their traditional domestic role was a way of protecting their husband's status and through that their own status' (Chaney 1980:51). Undertaking both domestic and paid labour as they do, it is scarcely surprising that working wives in particular, should have less leisure-time than their husbands.

In conclusion then, negotiations over the sexual division of labour within and outside the household may be resolved on the basis of tradition and patriarchy, or of rationality and the maximisation of economic interest; or both. As we have seen however, market forces tend to reinforce tradition in reducing the bargaining power of wives *vis-à-vis* their husbands. Whilst forces at work in the labour market towards growing flexibility for both men and women would seem to indicate the value of fitting men into gendered models, negotiations over the division of labour within the family appear to highlight gender differentiation. But just as men's labour market experiences are beginning to match women's, as flexible patterns of working spread through the labour market; so too may high unemployment and the changing structure of the labour market affect negotiations within the household and reduce the impact of traditional ideology in determining the outcome of these negotiations. This is precisely what the case studies of the Kidds and the Turners appear to show in Setting the scene 3. The next chapter will examine the empirical work which has taken place in this area. Chapter 5 will then argue that the process of negotiation between men and women over household work strategies requires a broader model than that of economic rationality, or patriarchy.

Part II

Re-articulation of the Divisions of Labour: Gender, the Family, and the Changing Nature of Work

Changing household divisions of labour

Mr and Mrs Briggs: no change from traditional rigid

The Briggs are a good example of a family in which there has been no change in the gender distribution of domestic work since Mr Briggs became unemployed. They are a family of four children; the oldest daughter aged 19 in full-time employment, an unemployed son, and 12-year-old twin sons. Mr Briggs was a red leader in the shipyards until he had been made redundant 9 months previously. He had always prepared the vegetables for Sunday lunch and put the meat in the oven. There was a good-humoured family dispute during the interview as to whether he ever did the washing-up after the Sunday meal. He had also always shared doing the decorating, but this was the limit of his domestic contribution. Mrs Briggs took a twilight shift cleaning job 6 years ago, initially to take her mind off her mother's death, 'but the money's nice once you start'. She also felt that the children were old enough by then – the twins were about 6 years old – and Mr Briggs was home from his job in time to look after them. The Briggs have therefore always had a traditional rigid organisation for domestic tasks, although Mr Briggs has long made a certain contribution to childcare.

Four years ago, Mrs Briggs took a day time cleaning job, working $12\frac{1}{2}$ hours a week in a school just down the road. By this time the older children could let themselves and the twins in, when they got home from school. The eldest daughter also helped her mother with making the main meal. When Mr Briggs lost his job, his wife's first response was to arrange to give up her own job, probably because what she earned was little more than her husband would receive for her and the children as supplementary benefit on top of his unemployment benefit. When asked whether there had been any differences in what he did in the house Mr Briggs said, 'I cannot think of any'. Mrs Briggs agreed that there had been none: 'We just went on the same, just went on regardless'. Mr Briggs meets the boys from school in the afternoon now, but they had been old enough to look after themselves before. True, he obviously enjoys being with his children, 'I just like carrying on with them. Playing football, or golf on the light nights. Birdwatching. Looking for golf balls', but then he had made such a contribution before.

The changes for Mr Briggs are that he is 'free all day, just lounging about, tinkering with the car'. He can take his wife to town in the car if needed, but otherwise, as he puts it: 'I'm just looking after the budgie'. Nevertheless, he has some extra activities outside the family; he visits an elderly neighbour in hospital three times a week and, as Mrs Briggs informed us, 'There's a lot of ladies on their own round here and when things go wrong it's usually this house they come to'. Perhaps Mrs Briggs giving up her own job so quickly reflects the continuing traditional domestic organisation in this household. Be that as it may, Mr Briggs provides an accurate assessment when he says: 'I just leave it to her. She just carries on the same. It's what it was before'.

Mr and Mrs O'Brien: some change to traditional flexible

Mr and Mrs O'Brien have changed from a traditional rigid to a traditional flexible form of organisation since Mr O'Brien lost his job through sickness 6 months ago. We have already met the O'Briens, and the reader may remember that Mrs O'Brien has been working for 13 years as a manufacturing operator on the twilight shift, having originally returned to work to pay for an extension to the house. Their children are both in work, a 22-year-old daughter and an 18-year-old son. Since he stopped work, Mr O'Brien has taken on a limited range of tasks, while Mrs O'Brien has significantly altered her routines and standards. Both indicate a change from traditional rigid to traditional flexible. Mrs O'Brien says that she has handed over the washing-up and cleaning the brasses to her husband; 'I try to find him something to do really because he just gets bored'. Mr O'Brien has also taken on responsibility for cleaning the bathroom – 'That's my pride and joy. When it's polished it shines out and it's lovely' – as well as helping with the hoovering and decorating since he stopped work.

Mrs O'Brien says that now her husband is not working he takes her to town more, and this alters her routine so that she does tasks at different times. Before, 'I had all the work done by midday'. She has also relaxed her standards, something that is very much part of a desire for companionship on both their parts. Having Mr O'Brien at home

doesn't make a great deal of difference apart from having him behind me back when I turn round. I could get on much quicker before. Now he's at home I get less work done, but I don't like to leave him on his own.

As Mr O'Brien puts it, 'Carol is company. If she was out at work all day, I think you'd go out of your mind'. It is interesting that both parents see their daughter and son doing less now that Mr O'Brien is unemployed. 'They helped more when he first came out of hospital, now they leave it all to me', says Mrs O'Brien, and her husband adds: 'I think you get put on more – they rely on us to get parts for the car or arrange the insurance'.

Mr and Mrs Smart: some change to more sharing

The Smarts are unusual in being the only family who had a sharing form of household organisation when they were both in work, so that when Mr Smart was made redundant they shared to a greater degree than before. The Smarts are a strongly Christian family who have four daughters, only one of whom – a 22 year old who works full-time as a shop assistant – is still at home. It appears that their Christian beliefs in sharing have always been put into practice in the household. Mr Smart was on shiftwork when the children were young, and if he was on 6.00 a.m. till 12 noon, he would come home and share looking after them. 'It's the love for each other that makes you do it,' he says. Mr Smart had experienced a 6-month spell of unemployment once before, and found that he did not want to get out of bed. Two years ago Mrs Smart took up work on school meals $29\frac{1}{4}$ hours a week, but there was a strong concept of sharing household tasks even when they were both working. Mr Smart took redundancy from the shipyards 10 months ago, and he has since been put on invalidity benefit as he is waiting for a hernia operation. Before this, according to Mrs Smart:

> I came in at three and Ronnie came in at five, and I had to *run* around tidying up and preparing the meal. Since Ronnie's not working I have more free time because I haven't got so much to do when I come in.

She also has less heavy shopping to bring in.

Mr Smart now goes round to his daughter's first thing every morning and takes his two grandchildren to school; since she also has a pre-school child, this is a great help to her. He then goes to church. 'It gets us out of bed' he says, though he enjoys it too. In his description of his typical day, Mr Smart then gives a fairly detailed account showing the responsibility that he takes for domestic matters.

> I come home, set the fire and put it on. Then done the potatoes. I had some soup for dinner. [Her mother made this.] I realised there was some ironing to do, so I done some ironing this afternoon. I

also hung up some clothes on the line. Then I hoovered round in time for Marlene to come back in,

after which he went to fetch the grandchildren again.

The increase in Mr Smart's responsibility is underlined when he says, 'Before I didn't have much idea. In the past I just went by Marlene's list, now I add to it.' Mrs Smart feels quite happy about her husband undertaking housework: 'I don't think it undermines a man in any way'. Nevertheless, her husband is aware of differences in standards and skills: 'I can't take Marlene's place as regards cleaning. A man does the top, whereas the woman gets into it'. It is worth mentioning that the sharing attitudes to housework extend to the children as well in this household. Mrs Smart says, 'I enjoy doing her things and having them ready for when she comes in and she wasn't expecting it. The attitude in here is that we enjoy doing things for each other'. Her husband then gives an example of their daughter putting the hot water bottle into her parents' bed. In sum, this is very much a change in domestic organisation made possible by the extra time that Mr Smart now has.

Mr and Mrs Archer: some change to sharing

The Archer family provide an interesting example of the change from a traditional flexible to a sharing arrangement, since the movement has been a gradual one over several years. The Archers have two adult sons, 19 and 17 years of age, who are both working; and a 12-year-old daughter. Mr Archer had been a fitter with the National Coal Board – as it was then – for 20 years before he was made redundant. Although he worked a lot of overtime until the late 1970s, there are indications that he has always done a few non-traditional domestic tasks. 'My husband was shown how to change nappies' says Mrs Archer, and when Mr Archer said that changing nappies was what he liked least about child-care, this confirmed that he actually did change them. 'Right from when the boys were little, you're hard pressed sometimes', points out Mrs Archer, 'so your partner more or less has to help'. Also, although Mr Archer does not like cleaning windows, he has always done it because his father was a window cleaner. Mrs Archer adds that 'We've always shopped for big items together, and chosen them between our'. It was because of her husband's overtime that Mrs Archer felt she could not take a job – I've always said I'd never let the kids be door step kids' – though as she says now, 'I've had years of being tied in the house and it gets you down'.

But when, three years ago, her husband was no longer doing overtime and her mother-in-law was living with them and able to meet the 9-year-old from school, she got a job $12\frac{1}{2}$ hours a week as a school cleaner. This was the point at which Mr Archer started to contribute to the meals: since Mrs Archer was at work she left a ready-prepared meal for her husband to put on. Then, in the spring of 1984 the pit dispute started and with the strike, says Mr Archer, 'I just got left with the lot' in terms of cooking the main meal. In fact cooking is now his favourite domestic activity, and Mr Archer takes some pride in what he has taught himself, for as his wife acknowledges, 'he learned hisself cooking'. He is now in charge of the main meal, he can make dumplings, and it's he who says, 'what are we going to have tonight?' Mrs Archer says she no longer has to worry over the main meal when she goes out to work at 3.30 p.m., pointing out that he would never have dreamed of doing the meal before the strike.

It was not merely a new routine for cooking, but for much else that was established during the year-long strike. Mrs Archer has never had to use her new shopping trolley since her husband now goes shopping with her. When they come in, he fries the mince straight away so that he can skim the fat off the top. When he was not in the house, Mr Archer just accepted that the work would have been done while now, 'Well away, it's time we got the sweeper on in here, and you start shifting chairs around'. Mrs Archer considers that since he has been on strike she does more or less half the work she used to, though there has not been that much of an increase in her free time, since they do many tasks together. As for overall responsibility, this too is shared for many tasks: 'a lot of them, because when you do them between you, nobody's in charge'.

Mr Archer was only back at work for 6 months when he got declared redundant, something that he was not unhappy with. (As for looking for work, 'I've got to admit I've been lackadaisical that way', though, 'eventually I'll have to'.) He has continued with the domestic pattern established during the strike, though some domestic tasks are still beyond him. 'Washing, that's one thing I would never do in the house. I wouldn't have a clue where to start'. In the last year his mother has died, but it is Mrs Archer who has taken over the washing-up that she used to do. Since his redundancy, Mr Archer has been doing a lot of decorating and has recently been replacing the bathroom suite. He is also a keen hill walker and rambler, and although Mrs Archer has been to the Lakes with him a few times, she has not been to the rambling club at the weekend since her mother-in-law died, because she does not like to leave her daughter. Mrs Archer thus takes on the domestic duties alone when her husband is out or away. In sum, Mr and Mrs Archer now have a sharing domestic organisation, and while Mrs Archer has a part-time job, Mr Archer has some absorbing leisure activities. These include a retrospective diary of all his walks: 'It's a bigger task than I thought, and writing is something new for me'; as well as the traditionally male activity of DIY.

Mr and Mrs Sterling: substantial change to exchange roles

The final case is of one of the most dramatic instances of change in the sample, that of the Sterling family. Interestingly, this family is the youngest one interviewed: Mr Sterling is 31, his wife 29, and they have three sons aged 9, 8, and 5. Mr Sterling has not worked since he lost his job as a labourer $5\frac{1}{2}$ years ago. When the three boys were small Mrs Sterling had a strict rota for herself for household tasks through the week, and this continued right up until she took a full-time job as a machinist $1\frac{1}{4}$ years ago. As she puts it, until that time 'he never thought of doing a thing'. But when they were both at home, Mr Sterling suffered from boredom: 'I didn't have anything to do when we were both in the house'. Mrs Sterling went back to work to find out if they'd be better off including the family income supplement she would receive. Though they didn't discuss who would do the housework and childcare, 'I just said, well, you'll have to help around the house, because I won't have time. He said he'd do this and that and the other'.

In fact, Mr Sterling has since been virtually in charge of all the housework and childcare through the week. As you might expect when she is out from 7.30 a.m. to 5.00 p.m., Mrs Sterling likes to see the children to bed at night and make them their supper: a hot drink and a biscuit before they go to bed. Mr Sterling plans and makes the main meal, but Mrs Sterling gets the shopping in on Friday afternoon since she finishes work early that day. She also hoovers right around and does the washing – 'she'll not let us do that' says Mr Sterling – on Saturday. Because of the teachers' dispute, which had been going on for some months, Mr Sterling takes and fetches the children four times a day to and from school. Small wonder that he says of his free time: 'Not a lot between 7.30 and 5 o'clock.' He reckons he has the same free time as he had when he was in employment, and as he says of undertaking casual work, 'not with three kiddies I couldn't'. I should perhaps mention that he also visits a lot of relatives – 'I travel all over the place' – doing 'turns' for them. His reasons for doing housework are that, 'I cannot expect the wife to come in and do it after a full day's work', and after all 'I'm in the house all day and I'm not going to sit on top of muck, I'm not going to neglect me bairns'. Yet he believes 'it should be the bloke out working and the women in the house'. A few days before I interviewed them, Mrs Sterling had given up her job since a recent time and motion study had reduced bonuses, and her earnings were lower. Her husband was looking for a job, and she was hoping to work part-time in the event of him finding employment. It was obviously too soon to see whether Mrs Sterling had taken up her former domestic duties again, but this family provides evidence of a strong pragmatic response to the exigencies of the labour market.

Chapter 4

Divisions of labour within the domestic economy and the process of change

Women and family work strategies

The previous chapter showed the extent to which theory has penetrated the black box of the household unit in recent years. This chapter will concentrate on the parallel growth of interest in empirical work which has looked within the household to assess patterns of work, consumption, and spending, and their distribution between household members. After a brief review of the empirical work to date, which indicates a shift in the focus of research from employment to the broader concept of work, I shall focus on my own Wearside study. For despite recent concern to examine the work that goes on inside families and its relation to employment in the formal economy, such studies have generally assessed the widespread traditional gender division in household work strategies. My own work focuses specifically on the role that men might take in the domestic and voluntary sectors when it is only their wives who are employed in the formal economy. My conclusions are at variance with recent researchers who are largely pessimistic about the possibilities for change in the gender division of labour under such circumstances.

An important first stage in research was to investigate the economic activities undertaken within the household and to compare them with work activities in the formal economy. Oakley's now classic works on housewives, did much to establish that domestic work and childcare were indeed work (Oakley 1974, 1976). Being a housewife, she demonstrated, involved a family role, and a feminine role, yet also a work role. She pointed out, however, that there are three major differences between housework and other kinds of work: that it is private, that it is self-defined and that 'its outlines are blurred by its integration in a whole complex of domestic, family-based roles which define the situation of women as well as the situation of housewife' (Oakley 1976:6).

Oakley's work was based on forty interviews, half with middle-class women, half with working-class women. The investment of women in their housework standards and routines was striking, and Oakley found that class differences were minimal. She also took a brief look at husbands' participation in both housework and childcare, asking specific questions on what husbands did. 'Only a minority of husbands give the kind of help that assertions of equality in modern marriage imply' (Oakley 1974, 1976:138). Some half of the working-class husbands were low in participation in both housework and childcare, though as she points out, the rating was a relative one, and social class differences are greater for housework than for childcare. Oakley concludes that 'Modern marriage may be characterised by an equality of status and "mutuality" between husband and wife, but inequality on the domestic level is not automatically banished' (Oakley 1974:146). In other words, marriages characterised by jointness in leisure activities and decision making are not necessarily those where husbands help with housework and children and vice versa.

Several commentators have pointed to a distinction between doing housework and childcare and being responsible for it. In particular, responsibility for the organisation of the household is identified as a female gendered task, with men making a minimum contribution here. Spending can thus be seen as a special responsibility task within a household, associated with managing the household economy, with women generally taking this on. As we have already seen, Hunt (1978) points to the housewife's concern to make money stretch, and her involvement in daily shopping adds to the concept of money as a general resource, rather than for herself. Indeed, money is generally unequally shared within the household, with male spending money as a protected category. Rigid arrangements over housekeeping money in homes with a sole male earner encourage female working. Such asymmetries in earning and spending money within households mean that men and women have differing perceptions of household needs, with a corresponding struggle over housekeeping money. Men's 'concerns were to secure the long-term well being of the household whilst the woman, because of her housekeeping role, was more concerned with immediate needs' (Morris 1987:93). The distribution pattern of consumption and spending patterns within the household has implications for the power relations within the household. Commentators have been at pains to demonstrate that control over household spending by women by no means ensures them a power position, but instead frequently results in wives putting children's and husbands' financial needs before their own.

There has been a recent arousal of interest in the relation between domestic work and employment. Several studies have been aimed at examining the way in which women combine their two jobs. I have already mentioned Judy Wajcman's (1983) study of the Fakenham women's co-operative where she is concerned to integrate the diverse aspects of women's domestic and work lives as they vary with the life cycle. She also examines the domestic division of labour and finds that although husbands perform certain domestic tasks, they are very different from those that women do in that they are neither routine nor continuous, but rather involve a few substantial tasks at intervals, often outdoors. Wajcman concludes that the domestic division of labour is doubly unequal, in that a greater share falls to the wife, and that her tasks are regarded as less skilled.

Frances Evans' (1984) study, undertaken on the Isle of Sheppey, shows the importance of specificity in relating women's domestic and labour market activities. She usefully suggests a typology of employment patterning for women who may take six possible employment routes over their lives. Women may be upwardly mobile, downwardly mobile, or immobile, and within each of these routes they may follow a continuous or an intermittent pattern. Similarly a fourfold typology can be used for domestic labour and the attitudes to it: on the one hand attitudes to it either change over the life cycle, or they do not; and women may have either positive or negative attitudes to their domestic work. The application of these two typologies to the life cycle of her interviewees allows Evans to conclude that there are very close links between women's attitudes to domestic labour, their domestic practices and their activity in the paid labour market. Domestic and employment spheres are closely related for women, and the domestic role is more complicated than is usually thought in that a woman's experience of employment and unemployment is mediated through her interpretation of the domestic role. Putting this another way, Marilyn Porter (1982) argues that when women enter the labour force they do so as migrants from the domestic domain.

What are the differences between the family work strategies of women and men? It is apparent that a major difference arises from the fact that many women with families are combining two jobs. Whilst the wife's employment career stops and starts, the husband's is continuous, and this asymmetry reflects the distribution of roles within the family and the gender division of labour. Perhaps the overriding characteristic of a woman's employment 'is that it functions as an adaptor or regulator within the family depending on circumstances in the family life cycle' (Barrère-Maurisson 1982:98). But how far does work in the home structure the decisions and choices of men as well as women in relation to their non-domestic lives? The family as an organisation needs to handle the performance of three basic functions: the man's paid employment, the woman's paid employment, and the children's need for supervision. 'The low level of pay for women in unskilled occupations confirms the traditional attitudes that childcare shall not cost anything while it also creates the necessity of free child care' (Stromsheim 1982:

26). Women exchange increased flexibility of working hours for low wages, but are also obliged to accept low wages and therefore to rely on free or very cheap childcare. Insofar as it is women who are employed as child minders and nursery nurses, cheap childcare is the rule, but even then it is only women employed in the primary labour market who can afford it.

So whilst it is important to relate women's domestic and labour market activities, there is an additional relationship between a wife's employment and her husband's role in childcare. Yeandle (1984) found that half of her respondents' husbands – whose wives were all in some form of paid employment – had taken part in caring for children, but some were just undertaking to be at hand, and it was only a minority who were willing to take on the labour of childcare. 'Being "at hand" when the children were small and being willing to take on some of the organisational tasks associated with older children, was all most women seemed to expect of their husbands' (ibid.:143). In other words, husbands were frequently crucial in enabling women to take on, in particular part-time jobs, but the husband's role in childcare was overwhelmingly related to the fact of his wife's employment. Half the women in Yeandle's sample reported men playing a significant role in terms of housework, usually washing-up, but also some household cleaning and meal preparation.

Finally, it is worth drawing attention to the fact that empirical studies to date indicate that women are not taking over as the main breadwinner, despite the pressures of economic recession and male unemployment. This is really scarcely very surprising given that women see themselves in the labour market on quite different terms from men. As Morris expresses it '*Her* employment decisions will largely be determined by *his* position in the labour market' (Morris 1987: 96). There are powerful constraints on women becoming the breadwinner in that women's often part-time wages, are unlikely to exceed supplementary benefit levels. One thus has two poles of workless and two-earner households, but in between there may be some households where both the man and the woman, the latter depending on the man, move in and out of employment. In households where the husbands are unemployed, the cost implications of low wages, childcare costs, travel costs and loss of benefit are enough to keep many women at home, even before ideological factors are taken into account.

Indeed, the majority of the unemployed – 55 per cent in 1980 – were dependent on means tested supplementary benefit (until the recent change to income support) rather than on unemployment benefit. Only the latter is payable as a right, provided sufficient contributions have been paid. Welfare intervention tends to freeze those out of work into unemployment (Mingione 1985:16) Under the British system of benefits, it is not merely individuals, but families, who tend to become frozen into unemployment. The incidence of unemployment amongst both husband and wife is surprisingly high. Eight per cent of wives of unemployed men are unemployed themselves, and a further 70 per cent are 'economically inactive' (*sic*). In contrast 3 per cent of women with employed husbands are unemployed and only 34 per cent are economically inactive. Thus 62 per cent of wives with employed husbands are working in the labour market, but only 22 per cent of those with unemployed husbands (General Household Survey 1985). Such figures are explicable in terms of two factors, which reinforce each other. The 'earnings rule' means that wives of men on supplementary benefit have for many years, faced pound for pound deductions from their earnings over £4. This situation remains broadly the same under the new income support system. Women's low levels of pay also mean that wives are unlikely to be able to earn more than their husbands' entitlement to benefit. This locks families into an unemployment trap. The trap can even operate on unemployment benefit as well, since large families often need to claim supplementary benefit to top up their income.

Men's domestic roles

As Oakley (1974) has pointed out, women are over-visible in the literature on the family, and the study of men's role is housework and childcare has, to date, been limited. True, several of the studies looked at so far have also been concerned to examine men's domestic roles, but have given it subsidiary importance. Taking gender seriously involves looking at men too. Joseph Pleck (1979) provides a useful framework of the three perspectives which can be used in investigating the division of family work. The traditional view is of course that the male role is as the family's economic support, therefore not involving housework. Here husbands exchange successful performance of the breadwinner role for provision of love, companionship, and household services. Such a perspective indeed confirms the traditional concerns of sociology, relating the woman to the family, and the man to employment. The exploitation perspective, which makes use of time-budget studies, shows the husband's contribution to housework as small, and moreover that its absolute size does not vary with the wife's employment. The empirical work arising from this perspective disproves the exchange theory on which the traditional perspective depends by showing that the sum total of paid and family work is heavier for women than for men.

   In contrast, the changing roles perspective looks at concrete strategies that might bring change about. This seems a very helpful approach to men's involvement in family work. As Pleck puts it 'From this point of view, an increased family role is the single most important

101

manifestation of change in contemporary society, just as increased labour force participation is probably the most important in the female' (Pleck 1979: 485). It is of course true that there is a lag between the rate of change of men's and women's roles – no doubt due at least in part to the strength of sexist ideology – but 'rather than view this discrepancy as a permanent feature of our society, it is more useful to view it as reflecting a transitional problem of adjustment' (ibid.: 485). On the basis of the empirical work done in Britain, there is disagreement as to whether roles are in fact changing or not, but let us pause to look at studies which take the exploitation perspective first of all.

Studies taking this perspective are in no doubt that it is the woman who is the chief worker in the household. 'If it has become conventional to refer to the married man as the "chief earner", it should be equally conventional to refer to his wife as the "chief worker"' (Pahl 1984:84). In a time-budget study concerned to look at twelve countries with urban populations beyond the minimum level of industrialisation, Robinson *et al.* (in Szalai 1972), found that the time devoted to paid work was very nearly doubled when housework and family care were added to formal work. Whilst men contributed 68 per cent of formal work time, they contributed only 22 per cent of housework time. Employed women spend half as much time on housework as their housewife sisters, but most striking is the work patterns for employed women on weekends. Whilst the employed man has leisure, and the housewife reduces her housework by 50 per cent, the employed woman doubles her time on housework on her day off. It is true that men on their days off do household *care* activities at a similar level to employed women (three-quarters of an hour a day), and that they double their *housework* activities on their days off too, but this only takes them up to half an hour a day, which is a drop in the ocean compared to women, since housework is a very large chore. The sum of employed women's socio-economic obligations, including formal work, household tasks, and travel, is greater than that of employed men on both workdays (49 per cent of a 24 hour day as against 43 per cent for men), and on days off (26 per cent for women, 16 per cent for men). Employed women also work more than housewives through the week – who only spend 38 per cent of their time on socio-economic obligations – but they do the same amount of work on a Sunday.

Whilst the exploitation perspective can be used to make overall generalisations about the relative contributions of women and men to household work, it is also useful to look at variations in inequality by class and by geographical area. Rosemary Collins' fieldwork was undertaken in the North East in Middlesbrough, and 'the interviews paid particular attention to men's domestic contribution and to the precise meaning of "sharing"' (in Close and Collins 1985:70). The fieldwork involved a postal survey of 1,000 households, followed by interviews with a sub-sample of fifty-seven. Her results showed women doing most domestic labour, but men giving varying degrees of help, and being highly involved in child-socialisation. Overall, her findings indicated a conjugal division of labour imbued with patriarchal relationships despite considerable participation by husbands/fathers. As with Wajcman, she found that men's domestic labour was different in kind from women's and in particular that whilst men may 'do' domestic labour, it is women who are responsible for it and that they organise, initiate, and complete domestic routines. She also noted that both men and women subscribe to sexist ideologies, and she found that the majority of skilled manual workers and unemployed men do more work in the home than middle-class men. She suggests that male unemployment may be the catalyst which will weaken the identification of women with domesticity in the future.

Amongst those who have taken the changing-roles perspective, two major possible causal factors have been identified: women taking up employment, or men becoming unemployed. Young and Wilmott (1973) and Rapoport and Rapoport (1978) both look to female employment as the precipitating factor, reaching relatively optimistic conclusions about the possibilities for gender roles becoming less traditional. There have been methodological criticisms of Young and Wilmott on the grounds that in concentrating on couples aged between 30 and 50 years old, there were likely to be fewer young children and elderly relations in households, with a correspondingly lower burden of domestic work. In contrast with later studies, they see marital symmetry as enhanced by the availability of part-time work for women, and argue that the power of feminism is such that the pattern of a single job for the husband and two jobs for the wife is a transitional phase in the development of the family. Evidence from the United States (see Voydanoff 1987) indicates that, since 1977 at least, the husbands of employed women spend more time in housework and childcare than the husbands of non-employed wives.

What of unemployment as a causal factor? Whilst they do not specify gender differentials, Pahl and Wallace in their examination of household work strategies in economic recession on the Isle of Sheppey are concerned with the relationship between employment, unemployment, and what they call self-provisioning (domestic work). They reach the interesting conclusion that employment and 'self-provisioning' go together, rather than being substitutes for each other. 'There is an indication that people *choose* to do this domestic work' (in Redclift and Mingione 1985:215). What this study highlights is that such a household strategy can be shattered overnight by redundancy or unemployment. It suggests that unemployment is likely to reduce the amount of domestic work undertaken in a household, but does not examine any changes in who does what.

There have been two pieces of British empirical work, as far as I am aware, that have specifically looked at the effects of male unemployment on the gender division of domestic work. Lorna McKee and Colin Bell interviewed forty-five families from Kidderminster in which the man was unemployed using a street sample method outside the unemployment benefit office, with a 6-month follow-up interview with forty-one of them. Before undertaking the research they saw male unemployment as heralding the convergence of the social worlds of men and women. In the event, they argue, it was as useful to look for continuities in the lives of unemployed people, and to identify the constraints against change. As they point out, 'unemployment of husbands does little to create new opportunities for women workers, but instead can be restrictive and perpetuate male/female inequalities in the labour market' (McKee and Bell 1984:24).

McKee and Bell (1984, 1985) were concerned to examine a wide range of effects of male unemployment: on attitudes to roles, on the allocation and control of money, on social life, and on domestic and maternal routines. They found a hardening and reinforcement of traditional attitudes, although they point out that their sample was a very young one, with young children, and that this stage in the life cycle is inevitably stressful. They also point out that male unemployment and its consequent financial stringency may actually involve an enlargement of the domestic role, particularly for the wife. Further, they make an interesting distinction between male and female based rationales for defining acceptable levels of male involvement in domestic tasks; the former relies on arguments on female nature, skill and expertise, while the latter argues for men's involvement in job search.

Lydia Morris looked at the re-negotiation of the domestic division of labour in the case of redundant male steel workers from Port Talbot in South Wales. As she points out, the sample was ideal in containing dependent children, making the domestic burden substantial, but the full psychological and economic impact of redundancy were not apparent at the time of interview. What is more, only two women out of the forty wives had become the main earner, and Morris suggests that 'In its broadest sense re-negotiation is dependent not on male unemployment, but on the availability of employment opportunities for women' (Morris 1983:14). Whilst she finds that both men and women feel strongly that it is the man's place to be the main wage earner, she notes that normative statements do not necessarily offer a clear guide to behaviour. In the course of her research, Morris identified three types of domestic division of labour: traditional rigid, traditional flexible, and renegotiated. Her overall conclusion was that 'We are witnessing a re-negotiation of certain details of everyday life within the household which is distinct from any serious re-negotiation of the underlying principles' (Morris 1983:15).

Unemployed men and family work on Wearside

A classification for the pattern of organisation of domestic tasks

I took a changing-roles perspective on men's involvement in family work for the empirical study on Wearside, by looking at the family situation most likely to bring change about: when husbands become unemployed, but their wives remain in employment. The first task in analysing the sample families already described in Setting the scene 1 was to establish a benchmark for the gender division of family work. It was important to formulate a classification for the pattern of organisation of domestic tasks, to be able to judge the extent of change in response to husbands not being at work. The process of evaluating the thirty taped interviews therefore started from a static analysis of the organisation of domestic tasks at the time of the interview, when the husband was not working whilst his wife was. In order to establish this classification, the average situation of the sample was looked at first of all. Typical examples of each type of classification have already been described in Setting the scene 3, before the theoretical discussion in the last chapter.

A benchmark for the gender pattern of family work was established by grouping specific household tasks and childcare according to whether they were gender neutral, or gender segregated, for the sample as a whole. For example, washing and ironing both showed strong gender differentiation, being mainly done by women, but hoovering was shared in a substantial number of families, and was gender neutral in that a similar number of wives and husbands always or mostly undertook it. This formed the basis for establishing a classification system for the patterns of the gender division of labour in the household. Distinctions were made between major tasks, such as washing or shopping, and minor tasks like making the breakfast or bed-making, and whether they were performed regularly or occasionally. Skilled tasks – for example making the main meal – unskilled tasks like washing-up, and tasks with a strong responsibility or managerial element, such as planning meals or handling the household's budget, were also distinguished.

Amongst the major regular, skilled tasks, there was a noticeable amount of sharing making the main meal, but very few men always or mostly undertook this. Washing and ironing both showed a strong gender differentiation, and were overwhelmingly women's tasks. Amongst the semi-skilled regular tasks, hoovering was gender neutral.

105

However, 'bottoming' was an almost exclusively female activity mentioned at some time in the interview by over a third of the families. Bottoming means pulling the furniture out and giving a thorough vacuum. As Mr Kelly put it 'she does it properly at the weekend', while his wife added, 'He does everything in the house until the weekend. Then I bottom. I do bedrooms and under beds what men don't think about, wash paintwork.' Household shopping was shared by about half the families, but in the other half it was women alone who did this task.

Washing-up was the only task which fell into the category of an unskilled major task. In nearly half the families it was shared, whilst slightly more men did the dishes alone than women. Only one task fell into the next category: that of a major occasional task. Decorating was also skilled. Again nearly half the families shared this task between husband and wife, but slightly more men did the task virtually alone than women. Minor tasks could be grouped together, first into tasks which tended to be shared and gender neutral, such as making breakfast, making other meals, preparing vegetables, bed-making, tidying-up, and dealing with pets. There were those which were done predominantly by women: if the task was done, packed lunches; dusting and polishing, sweeping, or washing floors; mending, which was very strongly female; shopping for big items, and window cleaning, again very strongly female. Finally, there were those done predominantly by men: gardening, mowing the lawn, household repairs, and taking the rubbish out.

Amongst the tasks which had a strong responsibility or managerial element in them, both planning meals and checking what was needed in the way of shopping were strongly women's work, the latter overwhelmingly so. Handling money was also gender segregated, being predominantly a woman's task, with no men at all being solely responsible, though in nearly a third of households, budgeting was shared. Childcare tasks should probably all be considered as containing a responsibility element, and they divided fairly easily into regular and occasional tasks. Unfortunately, as explained in Setting the scene 1, only half of the families had any childcare to do, and there was only one family with a pre-school child, so that some childcare tasks did not apply at all and others only applied to a few families. It seems worth suggesting that childcare overall will be a major task in any family with primary school age children, and this was the case for seven of the families. It was noticeable from the limited numbers for the various childcare tasks, that they appeared to be generally shared between men and women.

It was clear from this initial analysis of the performance of household tasks, that irrespective of any classification schema, there was a core of household (and to a lesser extent childcare) tasks, which were women's work. To some extent regardless of classification, there was gender differentiation of specific tasks within families too. For example only one husband always did the ironing, which was otherwise almost exclusively a female task; while only four wives made any contribution to the rather catch-all category of household repairs, tending to mention that they could mend a fuse or change a plug.

By considering the major regular tasks only, it was possible to establish a quantitative benchmark for the gender-differentiation of tasks: the five-task grading.[1] The aggregation of the performance of these tasks by the twenty-nine families[2] revealed a modal position in which three major tasks (the main meal, washing, and ironing) were done by the wife, whilst two tasks (hoovering and washing-up), were either shared or done by the husband. This 3:2 breakdown was thus the most frequently occurring pattern in the majority of households. The sixth major regular task, household shopping, in fact had a bi-modal character and as such did not contribute any further to the gender analysis of the regular tasks.

Taking this 3:2 pattern and giving it a value of 0, there could be deviations from the norm in either direction. If the husband did any of the three tasks done by women in the modal position (the main meal, washing, or ironing), a grade of +0.5 or +1 was given, depending on how many tasks he did. If on the other hand, the wife did all or almost all the five tasks, a grade of -0.5 or -1 was given on a similar sort of basis. It is of course noticeable that the two tasks that were most commonly done by men are less skilled than the three tasks most commonly done by women. Table 4.1 summarises the gradings allocated to the twenty-nine families who filled in the form. One must of course bear in mind that in the modal position, women were doing more major tasks than men, so that even in families with the least traditional score (+1) women were still undertaking a core of the major tasks. Five families fell into the modal position, with ten families on the more traditional side (scores of below 0) and fourteen on the less traditional side (scores of above 0). Once a more qualitative classification of families was developed, to include four main types of organisation of family work ranging from the least traditional form of exchanged roles through sharing and traditional but flexible to the most traditional form, that of traditional rigid, it became apparent that the benchmark based on the five-task grading did not entirely correspond. Table 4.1 nevertheless shows a fairly good twofold correspondence between the two traditional categories and families with scores below 0 on the one hand, and the sharing and exchanged roles categories and those with scores above 0 on the other.

Table 4.1 Grading of families based on five major regular tasks

Grading	Name of family	Bottoming, emergency, or large family factor	Classification finally allocated to	Number of families	% of families
+1	Kidd		Sharing		
	Kirby		Sharing		
	Mawson	B	Exchange roles	6	21
	Smart	B	Sharing		
	Sterling	B	Exchange roles		
	Toward	B	Exchange roles		
+0.5	Bewick	E	Trad. flexible		
	Bradshaw	B	Exchange roles		
	Dennis	B	Trad. flexible		
	Harris	E	Sharing	8	28
	Johnson	E, LF	Exchange roles		
	Kelly	B	Exchange roles		
	Laws	B	Sharing		
	White	B	Sharing		
0	Archer		Sharing		
	Giles	B	Sharing	5	17
	Hogg	E	Trad. flexible		
	Potts		Trad. flexible		
	Turner[1]	B	Exchange roles		
-0.5	Bolam	B	Trad. flexible		
	Carrick		Trad. flexible		
	Crowther		Trad. flexible	6	21
	Milne	LF	Trad. rigid		
	O'Brien		Trad. flexible		
	Tennet		Trad. rigid		
-1	Briggs	LF	Trad. rigid		
	Brown	E	Trad. rigid	4	14
	Coultard	E	Trad. rigid		
	Moody	E	Trad. rigid		

Key: 0 is when the wife does the main meal, washing, and ironing, while hoovering and washing up are shared or done by the husband.

If the husband does any of the main meal, washing, or ironing, a grade of +0.5 or +1 is given depending on how many stated.

If the wife does all, or almost all 5 tasks, a grade of -0.5 or -1 is given, again depending on how many stated.

Note: 1 The Turners' grading is skewed downwards because their daughter does all the washing up.

It is apparent then, that the five-task grading provides a simple means of estimating the appropriate classification for a family. Three other factors can be included in a quantitative judgement of the gender organisation within individual households which furnish an additional indication of the category that the family might fall into. Most importantly, the 'bottoming' factor tended to occur in families at the less traditional end of the scale. It will be remembered that bottoming is when the wife does a thorough clean-out of all or parts of the house, usually at weekends, or perhaps of an evening. This usually happened when the husband did an appreciable amount of hoovering, and in recognition – often by both husband and wife – of differing standards between women and men. It represents a process of accommodation to changes in the gender organisation of household work. The degree of bottoming varied largely with the extent to which less traditional husbands had taken on household cleaning tasks and was therefore a vestige of traditional gender segregation. So whilst Mrs Kelly mentioned bottoming, she also said she did not have to do much because 'he keeps the house in good order'. For Mrs Dent bottoming involved much more, and included 'the main jobs, like the bedrooms'. Bottoming of course was not mentioned in the more traditionally organised households: it did not apply in these cases, since the wife did it all anyway.

The other two factors do not have the same explanatory power as the bottoming factor, but tended to be associated with male justifications for the status quo in traditional families. Taking the 'emergency' factor first, this was when husbands took on all the domestic or childcare tasks when their wives were unable to do them, whether because of having a baby, illness, or being in hospital. Six families referred to the fact that the husband took over in such emergencies, but it would appear that although some learning might take place, this was rarely translated into a more regular contribution once the emergency was over. On the whole, the presence of the emergency factor tended to confirm that the family was at the more traditional end of the scale. The same was true of the large family factor. This was where daughters – rather than sons it would appear – helped their mothers with domestic or childcare tasks, thus relieving them of some of the domestic burden, but at the same time justifying their fathers in not doing very much. For example in the Briggs family, the 19-year-old daughter – who was incidentally in full-time employment – helped her mother out with meals, washing-up, and hoovering and dusting.

Whilst the five-task grading gave a general picture of the appropriate classification for a family, a far wider range of factors needed to be taken into account to provide a more thorough and complete classificatory schema. Some eight factors in all were involved. Three of these related to time and quantity: relative quantity of work done by husband

and wife, relative amounts of free time, and hours of paid work for wives. Quality was assessed through standards and routine, by the skill element in tasks and by their gender specificity. Responsibility and ideological perceptions of roles were the last two factors taken into account. Once more, it is important to be aware that irrespective of any classification schema, there is gender differentiation in families. In other words, there was a core of household, and to a lesser extent childcare, tasks which were women's work. This applied not merely to quantity of work but also to its quality, including skills; and to respons- ibility for work. It is for this reason that the term 'role-reversal' was not used for the least traditional families, since the implication is that the traditional roles have simply been completely reversed. This did not happen in any of the sample families, but what was apparent was a marked differentiation between families in terms of the degree of gender segregation in the organisation of family work, amply justifying a fourfold classification. Case study examples of each category of house-hold organisation have been given in Setting the scene 3, but let me now turn to the characteristics of each type of household organisation, starting with the most traditional. The differences between each are summarised in Table 4.2.

In the traditional rigid form of organisation, the husband performs almost no domestic tasks apart from some predominantly male minor tasks such as gardening or mowing the lawn. He might make a limited contribution to a narrow range of other tasks such as peeling vegetables on a Sunday, or washing-up occasionally. For example, the interview had barely started when Mr Briggs said 'Ask us about the Sunday dinner', and he provided a detailed job specification of his sole non-traditional domestic task: preparing and putting on the Sunday vegetables and meat. The traditional rigid category is exemplified in a five-task grading of -1 or -0.5, but the emergency factor may be present in that the husband takes on the domestic tasks in an emergency. Turning to his wife, she will do her housework either before or after she goes out to work, and she may well be very busy with household chores at the weekend.

For Mrs Briggs Sunday is the busiest day of the week, 'It always has been – I seem to be in the kitchen from morning till night.' Her burden may be relieved by help from daughters – the large family factor – or indeed she may have decided to give up her job. She may well be in employment for relatively short hours. She does not mention bottoming since she does the vast bulk of household tasks herself anyway. Her household routine tends to respect her husband, in that she will try not to disturb him even though he may be around all day. As Mr Briggs says 'If I just fancy a cup of coffee or a biscuit, she does that'. If the husband does make a small contribution, it is likely to be at his convenience.

Table 4.2 Characteristics of the four types of household organisation

Household organisation	5 task grading	Bottoming, emergency, large family	Major tasks	Minor tasks	Household routine	Responsibility	Wife's employment	Gender segregation: practice and ideas
Traditional rigid	-1 or -0.5	E and LF may be present, not B	The wife; husband may help with washing up	The husband does a few	The wife has routine, including weekend. Respects the husband	Wife	Short hours. May have given up	Strong, including traditional ideas
Traditional flexible	-0.5 or 0		The husband may do washing up, and may help with decorating or shopping	The husband does some non-traditional ones	The wife has routine, including at weekend	Wife	Range of hours worked	Somewhat less strong. Some see importance of sharing
Sharing	0 or above esp. +0.5 or +1	The wife may bottom at weekend	Some are shared/may be done by the husband	A range are shared	The husband may articulate clear routine	The husband takes on elements, but not much	Substantial: around 20 hrs, not full-time	Less strong. Strong sharing ideology
Exchange roles	+0.5 or +1	The wife may bottom	The husband does/shares a range with wife	The husband does substantial range	The husband has clear routine	The husband has substantial responsibility especially during week	Full-time breadwinner. The husband may help	Most gender congruent, but residual elements of tradition, especially in ideology

Traditional rigid households have a strong gender segregation in practice and this may be reinforced by the husband and wife holding to strong traditional views of gender roles. As Mrs Briggs puts it: 'We more or less carry on the old way, like they did years ago, not now they don't do they?'

In the traditional flexible household, the wife may still be busy at the weekend or regularly do housework before or after going to work. Mrs Dennis for example, bakes, makes dinner, and does the ironing on Sunday 'ready for work Monday'. She may still not have much free time. Her husband on the other hand will undertake some non-traditionally male minor tasks. Of the five major tasks, he will only do the washing-up, though he may help with some others such as decorating or shopping. The husband may well be very clear that there are some tasks that he will not do. 'I'd never do dusting' declares Mr Carrick, 'A man with a duster, I'd be wearing a pinny next!' The five-task grading of such a family is likely to be -0.5 or 0, and gender segregation is somewhat less strong than in the case of traditional rigid families. In terms of ideology it is possible that there may be declarations of the importance of sharing – 'It's teamwork that counts' says Mr Carrick – but they are not put into practice any more than the above indicators would suggest.

In the case of sharing households, a range of tasks including some of the five major tasks are shared between the husband and wife, or may even be done by the husband. There are nevertheless limits on what the husband does, and the wife may well bottom at the weekend. The grading of such families on the five-tasks will be 0 or above, most likely either +0.5 or +1. It may be that the husband does not take on very much responsibility, for he may do what his wife suggests he should do, but he will probably take on some elements of responsibility. According to Mrs Kirby: 'Why he always does the stairs down for me and I do the rest'. Some wives in this category will argue that since they share tasks, nobody is actually in charge. Quality of work may well have become an issue for the husband as well as the wife, so that, for example, the husband may articulate a clear routine for the tasks that he does. Both he and she may accept the need for standards to be maintained by her undertaking more or less bottoming. This is nevertheless a far cry from the household routine of the traditional rigid wife who tries to respect the needs of the unemployed husband for privacy and quiet. The sharing organisation often goes with a strong ideology of the importance of sharing domestic tasks between husband and wife. 'I think it would be more loving if men did more housework' says Mr Laws, and although in practice it is not by any means a 50:50 equality, there is nevertheless a noticeable element of sharing. 'It doesn't matter what we want, we shop together' insists Mrs Kirby. The sharing household often has an ideo-

logy of mutual support and company. It is interesting that other commentators do not seem to have come cross this category of domestic
organisation in their field work. This may be because they have concentrated on the unemployed status of men, and it is noticeable that
almost all the women in sharing families do a substantial amount of paid
work.

The fourth and final category is that of exchanged roles. Here the
husband does a substantial range of tasks, either alone or shared with his
wife, whilst she is either the family breadwinner or has more or less
full-time employment. The five-task grading in such a family is either
+0.5 or +1, indicating that the wife does less than the norm. In de-
scribing her typical day, the wife may have little to say about domestic
matters, concentrating rather on what happened at work. She may well
feel that she has handed over the bulk of the housework to her husband
– 'He became the housewife' is how Mrs Toward puts it – though she
may still bottom and do extra tasks either in the evening or at weekends.
Her husband on the other hand will probably describe or mention more
tasks than other men and be more open and articulate on household
matters. He may well describe his household routine in some detail, and
will have substantial responsibility for the household, at least through
the week. 'When they'd go to school and she'd gone to work I started in
here, front room, kitchen, bathroom then upstairs. . . .she didn't have to
ask' was Mr Toward's typical day. He may also perform an essential
function: for example by picking children up and bringing them home
for lunch – the teachers' dispute was on throughout the interview period
– or by being at home when they get home from school. Husbands may
also undertake tasks that men often or usually do not do. Finally, the
husband may help with aspects of his wife's job, or take her to work.

In terms of roles, there may be some reluctance in principle for wives
taking on the breadwinner role and husbands undertaking household and
childcare tasks, but not in practice. Husband and wife may well express
gratitude towards each other: he for her bringing in the wage, she for his
role in the running of the house. In some cases there is indeed a
noticeable breakdown of gender stereotypes. 'As far as I'm concerned it
made him more of a man. A man isn't a macho man with a hairy chest
and a gold medallion. It's how he lives his life' says Mrs Toward. An
exchanged-role organisation implies just that; there has been some
exchange of roles between husband and wife. There will still be residual
elements of tradition, which may even be strong in certain respects,
perhaps particularly in terms of responsibility for money. For example,
Mrs Toward would not let her husband sort out the washing or do the
ironing: 'I didn't really trust him – I suppose it was wrong of me'.
Nevertheless this form of organisation involves a much looser gender
segregation than the others.

Table 4.3 Classification of the sample families

Classification	Name of family	'Bottoming', 'emergency', or 'large family factor'	Hours of employment for wife	5-task grading	Age of youngest child	No. of families	% of families
Exchange Roles	Bradshaw	B	FT	+0.5	Secondary		
	Kelly	B	32	+0.5	Primary		
	Mawson	B	32	+1	Adult		
	Sterling	B	FT	+1	Primary	7	23
	Toward	B	FT	+1	Primary		
	Turner	B	FT	0	Secondary		
Partial Exchange	Johnson	E, LF	15	+0.5	Primary		
Sharing	Archer		12½	0	Secondary		
	Kidd		20	+1	Secondary		
	Kirby		20	+1	Adult		
	Harris	E	18	+0.5	Adult	8	27
	Laws	B	22½	+0.5	Adult		
	Smart	B	29¼	+1	Adult		
Reluctant Sharing	Giles	B	20	0	Adult		
	White	B	20[1]				
Traditional Flexible	Bewick		22¼	+0.5	Adult		
	Carrick		18	-0.5	Adult		
	Crowther		25½	-0.5	Adult		
	Hogg	E	7½	0	Adult	8	27
	O'Brien		20	-0.5	Adult		
	Potts		4½	0	Adult		
Reluctant Flexible	Bolam	B	17½	-0.5	Primary		
	Dennis	B	FT	+0.5	Adult		
Traditional Rigid	Briggs	LF	12½[2]	-1	Secondary		
	Brown	E	5[3]	-1	Adult		
	Coulthard	E	4	-1	Adult		
	Milne	LF	16	-0.5	Preschool	7	23
	Moody	E	14[4]	-1	Adult		
	Tennet*		12½	-0.5	Primary		
	Ward[5]		mornings	n.a.	Secondary		

Notes: 1 Mrs White gave up her job in July 1985.

2 Mrs Briggs gave up her job in June 1985.

3 Mrs Brown worked 16 hours a week until February 1985.

4 Mrs Moody took up her second job of 10 hours a week in January 1986.

5 This is a classificaion based on the limited information from the doorstep interview.

*This family is traditional flexible for childcare.

There was an almost uncannily even distribution of the sample families into the four types of household organisation, as Table 4.3 shows. Very nearly a quarter fell into each category. This is of course a classification for when the husband is out of work and the wife is in employment, and such a structure of family employment makes the sample families very different from those in the field work done by either Morris (1985) or McKee and Bell (1985). It is nevertheless very striking that half the sample had distinctly non-traditional forms of organisation for family work, while only a quarter of the sample fall into the traditional rigid category.

There was a wide variation in the form of domestic organisation within the sample, and this static classification indicated a strong link between organisational form and the hours of work of wives. Exchanged roles are associated with full-time work, and indeed only in one case where the wife works more than 30 hours is this not the form of organisation. It is perhaps rather surprising that exchanged-role families also seem to be characterised by dependent children. This is possibly because the cost of bringing up a family encourages the wife to change to a breadwinning role, while at the same time the volume of domestic work forces the husband to undertake it. In the sharing category, the wives show a substantial commitment to the labour market by working around 20 hours or more, but they do not work full-time, and indeed full-time work would be incompatible with the sharing practice and mentality of this group. On the other hand, if wives work less than 20 hours, there is not such an incentive for husbands to participate in family work. The traditional flexible category shows no association with hours of work of wives, and the group incorporates women working a wide range of hours. It is not surprising that the category with limited modification of traditional roles should be found across a wide range of commitment to the labour market by women. Turning finally to the traditional rigid group, there is again an association with hours, this time with very low hours of work. This may not be apparent at a first glance at Table 4.3, but this group has actually experienced a lot of recent change in hours. A system of domestic organisation in which the husband does almost no domestic tasks also tends to mean that the wife will only take on a small role in the labour market. This is indeed the traditional gender role-segregation.

Thus hours of work of women can be seen as a direct representation of their economic power, and the more economic power women have, the more their husbands will be prepared to take on what is traditionally women's work. Pragmatically, the longer the hours that women undertake paid work, the shorter the time they have to be domestic, while husbands who are not working have no such time constraint and can correspondingly take on the domestic role. The association found between forms of household organisation and wives' hours of work, vindicated the original hypothesis that women being in paid work when their husbands were not, would tend to encourage a more gender congruent division of household tasks. Whilst some might criticize my conclusions on the grounds that even the most non-traditional form of organisation, exchanged roles, is not role-reversal, it is important to keep in mind that role-reversal is simply the obverse of the traditionally rigid division of labour between the sexes. In other words, complete role-reversal is as inflexible as its polar opposite, a traditional rigid organisation.

Some, relatively limited information was available from the interviews about the contribution made by children to family work, but it is important to recall that the seventy children presently living in the sample families covered a very wide age range, and that even amongst the thirty-seven adult children there was the difference between the employed and the unemployed to consider. Two general conclusions can be drawn from the indications of the tasks that daughters and sons undertook. First, there were distinct gender differences in children's contributions to household tasks, with noticeably more daughters than sons helping with tasks. Second, in general children made a very small contribution to household tasks, and it was only in six families that children helped with a range of tasks, rather than one or two at most. A large family factor operated in three families, where daughters helped their mothers out to a noticeable extent.

When the responses of parents were taken into account, it was not surprising that children did not do much, for on the whole parents had very low expectations of them. There were gender differences in expectations, with daughters usually expected to do more than sons. Children were however caught in a catch-22 situation, since despite low expectations, a substantial number of families expressed dissatisfaction with how little their children did, and at the same time there was little evidence of parents attempting to teach their children to do things around the house. Whilst the data for children was limited, the available evidence would seem to suggest that in terms of current practice and expectations, the prospects for change in gender roles is not very high. The recent changes in gender practice in the older generation which we shall be looking at in a moment, did not appear to be mirrored in what their children did. The present generation of young people look almost as ill-prepared for change as their parents! This is an area where more empirical work deserves to be done.

Changes in the gender organisation of households

What of the extent to which families had changed their household organisation in response to husbands no longer working? Change is a difficult concept to grasp, and it is certainly not easy to provide any measure of it. Ideally a longitudinal study should be used, or a life history approach, for it is certainly not easy to get at change in a single-interview situation. Nevertheless, within the resources and time constraints of the project, sufficient indicators of change were available to establish the degree of change in household organisation that had taken place since the husband had lost his job. Such indicators fell into four main categories: those relating to who undertook the whole range of household tasks, who undertook specific tasks, the effects of change on the wife – in terms of more free time, for example – and changes in responsibility or routines. These indicators were used as a first stage in establishing a typology of change, but information from the whole interview was added, and an overall judgement was made of the extent of change within each household. Four types of change were identified: regressive, no change, some change, and substantial change, and case studies of each have been given in Setting the scene at the start of this chapter. Some change will occur when a family moves one classification towards a less traditional form of organisation, while substantial change is when the family has moved two classifications.

Regressive change usually goes with the husband finding some sort of substitute for paid work. This may be outside the household and involve visiting relatives, going to the club a lot, or participating in the complementary economy, this latter being overwhelmingly an exchange economy. It could also be within the household, but if it is, the husband will occupy himself with traditionally male tasks: DIY, repairing appliances or fixing up the car. Either substitute for paid work involves the husband in developing his own routine separately from that for household chores, though he could alternatively become very depressed.

From the point of view of the wife, regressive change means a change for the worse in that she finds her husband in the way, or that it means more work for her. According to Mr Coultard 'I don't think she's got much free time, looking after me and the two lads'. Under these circumstances the wife may rely on her daughters to relieve the burden on her: the large family factor. It is interesting that throughout the interview with Mr Coultard, his 18-year-old son was baking a cake whilst his wife was preparing the meal. Additionally, the wife may actually prefer her husband to be out since it reduces arguments, or she may herself go out more to prevent them. Finally, regressive change may be associated with the wife having had more paid work in the past.

The characteristics of the no-change category by their nature require little discussion. It is likely that there will be no change when the family is in any case at the traditional end of the spectrum, though habit and lethargy may contribute to non-movement.

There are a number of key characteristics for the cases where there is some change. Generally the contribution from the husband is seen in terms of 'helping' or perhaps 'mucking-in', and it may be that he has always helped, but now helps more. 'You've always helped in the house haven't you?' says Mrs Kidd, who sees her husband as 'being good in the house'. On the other hand, the husband may be bored and so takes on a number of domestic tasks. Mr White, for example, comments that there is nothing he likes best about housework: 'I just do it from boredom'. The husband may have done nothing in the way of housework before because his hours of work did not allow it. As Mrs Bolam comments of her husband: 'It was just a case of work and bed'. For some couples unemployment is an opportunity to put a principle of sharing into practice, whilst for others there has been a shift in attitudes to roles, as well as in practice. Mr Bewick thought that hoovering and hanging out the washing were women's work before he became unemployed. There are also some features which will prevent more change taking place: the husband may be sufficiently ill to prevent him doing more, or he may be lying in bed, or it may be that the wife does not let her husband take on any more tasks.

Substantial change, a shift in two classification categories, will almost inevitably be a shift to exchanged roles. Such change frequently involves the recognition that the wife has become the breadwinner. On the one hand substantial change often means the wife becomes more flexible over housework standards and being tolerant of her husband's. As Mr Sterling says of his wife's former rota for cleaning tasks: 'She does that. I couldn't be chewed on with it.' On the other, it may mean that the husband either gets trained by his wife for the various household tasks, or that he goes through a process of teaching himself. 'Now I can tackle anything', says Mr Turner, 'have a go at them.'

If families are at the traditional end of the scale with regard to the domestic division of labour, the most likely changes will be traditional rigid and regressive, traditional rigid with no change, or traditional rigid to traditional flexible. The no-change category is certainly only likely to occur in traditional rigid families. It is unlikely that there will be a shift from traditional rigid to sharing since the former usually involves a traditional attitude to roles which is not present in sharing families. The shift to sharing then, is likely to be from a traditional flexible family organisation. On the other hand the movement to exchanged roles can be from either traditional flexible or traditional rigid because of the objective factor that the wife works long hours. One would not normally expect a shift from sharing to exchanged roles, since sharing is very unlikely to be possible unless the husband is unemployed.

Table 4.4 provides a summary of the degree of change showing the type of change that has taken place in household organisation for each family. In nearly half the families there has been some change (eight from a traditional rigid to a traditional flexible form of organisation, five from traditional flexible to sharing), and there has been substantial change in a further six families, with three families moving from traditional flexible to exchange and two from traditional rigid. In other words, twenty families (nearly 70 per cent of the sample) have undergone change towards a less rigid division of labour within the household, while only seven families (less than a quarter) have not, although three families could not be assessed, either because they had been unemployed for such a prolonged period or because they had only recently married. This is a striking indication of the responsiveness of the gender organisation of households to the non-employment of husbands, although two reservations must be kept in mind. In a few families change took place in response to other circumstances as well as the husband's unemployment, though the Sterlings were in fact the only family in which the husband's unemployment categorically did not precipitate change. In this case it was Mrs Sterling taking on a full-time job, though Mr Sterling's unemployment was still a precondition for his high level of participation. Secondly, it has already been emphasised that even the change to exchanged roles means that there is still a core of household and childcare tasks undertaken by the wife.

Understanding the process of change proved to be very much a matter for individual case study, and some examples are given both in Setting the scene for this chapter and for the next, giving some indication of the wide range of variables which can influence the process. These case studies show that variations in the gender distribution of housework and childcare are an individual experience for each family, confirming the validity of a methodological approach based on in-depth interviews with a small number of families. Change in a non-traditional direction was not simply in terms of an extra volume of work done by men. There were also increases in the amount of free time for women, and often an increase in the responsibility taken by men. Men had also developed housework and childcare skills as well as adopting standards and routines for housework in come cases. Whilst men tended to take on tasks which are more generally done by men or shared with their wives, there was also some reduction in the gender segregation of tasks.

To summarise on the process of change, time available proved crucial to the gender distribution of family work precisely in the double sense that was assumed when the project was initiated. On the one hand, unemployment is a precondition for men taking on more work than is involved in a traditional flexible form of household organisation. If the wife is employed, male unemployment does tend to lead to a positive change in gender distribution and only in a minority of cases will there be no change or a regressive change. On the other hand, the amount of

119

Table 4.4 Individual families and the degree of change

Type of change	No. of families	% of families	Names of families	Length of non-employment for husband months (m)/ years (y)	Length of employment for wife months (m)/ years (y)	Wife's hours of work
TR and Regressive	3	10%	Brown	6y	23y	5
			Coulthard	1y	6y	4
			Milne	7y	6m	16
TR No Change	4	13%	Briggs	9m	4y	12½
			Moody	3y	10y	14⁴
			Tennet	6m	5y	12½
			Ward[1]	1y	12y	mornings
Some Change TR→TF	14	47%	Bewick	1½y	13y	22¼
			Bolam	11m	9y	17½
			Carrick	4y	12y	18
			Crowther	6y	15y	25½
			Dennis	2½y	12½y	FT
			Hogg	3y	16y	7½
			O'Brien	6m	13y	20
			Potts	7y	12y	4½
Sh→More Sh			Smart	10m	2y	29½

Category	n	%	Name			
TF→Sh			Archer	5m	3y	12½
			Harris	5½y	7y	18
			Kidd	2y	2½y	20
			Laws	8m	3y	22½
			White	10m	2½y	20
Substantial Change TR→Sh			Giles	3y	15y	20
TF→Ex	6	20%	Bradshaw	2½y	2y	FT
			Kelly	4y	6y	32
			Turner	11m	5½y	FT
TR→Ex			Sterling	5½y	2½y	FT
			Toward	11m	1½y	FT
Non-assessable	3	10%	Johnson[2]	19y	7m	15
			Kirby[3]	2y	14y	20
			Mawson[2]	13y	12y	32
Totals	30	100%				

Notes: 1 Probable: this was the doorstep interview.
2 Unemployed for long period
3 Recently married.
4 10-hour job only taken up in January 1986

change will tend to be related to the number of hours that wives work. The response of Wearside men to no longer being in paid work demonstrates a substantial degree of flexibility with respect to domestic and childcare tasks. In particular, it suggests that men are making a pragmatic response to an overall family work situation in which, if the wife is also in paid work, her husband is likely to take on at least some of the domestic duties. This is a far cry from the Andy Capp image of the North East. In order to gain further understanding of how unemployed men and their families adjust to change, it is important to locate the family and its work strategies within the wider economy, and this is the concern of the next chapter.

The influence of tradition and of the state benefit system

Mr and Mrs Milne: regressive change and traditional ideas reinforced by the state

The Milnes are a very large family with six children ranging from 3 to 19 years old. Prior to his stopping work seven years ago through sickness, Mr Milne had worked as a plater in the shipyards for many years. This was a very traditional family and as Mr Milne puts it, before he stopped work 'I thought [childcare] was women's work and I still think it's women's work, not because I'm a chauvinist but I think women are better at it and kids prefer their mothers anyway'. When he did stop work, Mrs Milne found herself with an increased workload: 'He sits about and leaves a mess. He's always in the bath, he never empties it and he leaves the cupboard doors open'. There is a patriarchal element present when Mr Milne says 'I sometimes ask her to use more imagination in cooking', but he too acknowledges that he makes work: 'I like cooking, but I leave a mess'. Since he stopped work Mr Milne goes out a lot, and he's secretary at his local social club, for which he is paid a small amount.

Now that Mrs Milne has taken a job as a cook 16 hours a week, a neighbour minds their 3-year-old daughter and takes her to playschool. If she wants her husband to look after the little one, Mrs Milne has to ask him. Indeed even this is not necessarily enough as Mr Milne admits in his description of a typical day.

> My wife brought a cup of tea and the paper up at five to nine before she left for work, and asked if I'd stay in and get the bairn from the neighbour about ll.30 a.m. I got up about 10.00 a.m. and watched a video. The eldest kids came back from school at 12.30 p.m. and I sent them to pick the bairn up.

In fact Mrs Milne relies a lot on her children to help her, especially the 14 and 13-year-old daughters. 'The bairns have always helped. It's very rarely I wash or tidy up. I don't have to ask'. This large family factor provides a rationalisation for Mr Milne: 'I think I'd be more involved in household tasks if it wasn't for the kids being able to do it'. Typically for the traditional rigid family, an emergency factor is also present: when Mrs Milne is ill, her husband takes on all the tasks. 'If I've got to do something, like when she's in bed, I'll do it, no arguments' remarks Mr Milne. It was the fact that Mr Milne went on to invalidity benefit 2 years ago that made his wife go back to work: 'I've always wanted a job. When he was on the dole I couldn't get a job 'cos they'd take the money off yer, but when he's on sick I'm allowed to work'. It was certainly not her husband's domestic contribution that encouraged her, since he made more work; but her domestic work has declined, partly because her daughters help more, partly because, as Mr Milne points out, the children are older now.

Mr and Mrs Giles: reluctant sharers

It is unexpected to find a family that has changed from a traditional rigid to a sharing form of household organisation, but it becomes understandable in the context of the Giles being 'reluctant' sharers. The family is a large one: six children altogether, though only two daughters – aged 19 and 18, neither of whom has ever worked – remain at home now. Mr Giles spent 29 years in the shipyards before he was made redundant 3 years ago. It is apparent that in the past Mr Giles did very little indeed in the house, though when Mrs Giles took a twilight cleaning job at the local hospital from 4.00 p.m. to 8.00 p.m. he took over minding the children from the neighbour when he got in from work.

Five years ago Mrs Giles got the chance of working mornings for 20 hours a week 'I preferred having the rest of the day free, and the girls were grown up'. It was at this stage, when both she and her husband were working in the daytime that her daughters gave Mrs Giles a good deal of help. As she says, now 'they don't help as much as they used to when he was working. They used to help me with little things, keep their rooms tidy, put the washer on without me asking'. But when Mr Giles was made redundant there was a substantial change. When asked about this, Mr Giles declared 'Aye, I do it all'. Mrs Giles now sees her husband as responsible: 'He's just completely took over. I just keep my mouth closed now'. So, for example, Mr Giles does all the vacuuming and washing-up as well as a fair number of minor tasks, although Mrs Giles still bottoms. 'She does the polishing and that properly at the weekend'. Mr Giles has taken up housework to fill his time: 'I just like to do it. There's nothing else to do. It takes up time.'

However, this is unwelcome for his wife who had a very well-developed routine while he was working.

> To me I like to do the jobs when I'm ready to do them and in the
> way I want them done; since he's in the house all day he's doing
> it. I won't interfere . . . but it doesn't get done the way I wanted it
> done.

As she says 'If he was working he wouldn't be doing it'. Mrs Giles is
not merely reluctant to hand over her role as a housewife, she is also
reluctant to take on the role of breadwinner.

> Well, I'm not over the moon about it [his unemployment] because
> in the first place I went out to work to help, to get extras and now
> I feel as though I'm working to pay for necessities whereas before
> I had a bit of me own independence.

In this family the changes have been initiated by Mr Giles himself, and
Mrs Giles has reluctantly accepted the situation. It is finally worth
mentioning that Mr Giles is in turn resentful of his daughters not merely
because they now do nothing in the house, but also because he has very
recently gone off invalidity benefit. 'The point is, there's the two girls
who have never worked and they're getting more than me. I've worked
29 years in the shipyards . . . . It's the system that's wrong. You can't
beat the system.'

Mr and Mrs Bradshaw: substantial change, despite state disincentives and traditional views

The Bradshaws are an example of a family which has changed from a
traditional flexible to an exchanged-roles form of organisation. Mr
Bradshaw spent 23 years as a butcher until his employer went bankrupt
with a divorce settlement, and he loved his job despite the low pay. As
a child his mother was not very reliable so that he and his brother learned
to fend for themselves from an early age. When they were first married
Mr and Mrs Bradshaw therefore decided that they would share the
domestic tasks, at least till the children came along. They now have two,
a 15-year-old daughter and a 13-year-old son, and since their birth Mr
Bradshaw has always helped with the housework on a Sunday, something that is most unusual for the men in the sample. When her son was
about two years old, Mrs Bradshaw started work again on the twilight
shift of a mail order firm, and this is why she says: 'he's always helped,
taking on nightly duties'. Yet Mrs Bradshaw is emphatic that 'I've been
the main one [to look after the children]. Malcolm's been there to stand
by'. She has always preferred to punish the children herself since she
feels that fathers should not be feared by their children.

It was just over 2 years ago that Mr Bradshaw got made redundant,
and only 4 months or so later that Mrs Bradshaw got full-time work as a

warden in sheltered accommodation for the elderly. The family therefore moved from Sunderland to Washington into the house that went with Mrs Bradshaw's job. Because the two events are so close together it is difficult to tell which had most effect on the changes that have since taken place. Possibly because he has always been helpful in the house, both Mr and Mrs Bradshaw seem to have a fairly modest view of the amount of change that has taken place, but Mr Bradshaw points out that he now does housework through the week. Mrs Bradshaw says that she has 'much more free time now even though I'm working full-time, because he does most of the household tasks', although she occasionally does some housework in the afternoon when she's finished work. 'He does the housework while I do the hobbies' she adds.

For Mr Bradshaw it's 'very belittling really. A man shouldn't do housework. I'll do it, that's it.' Of the major tasks he now shares four of them (washing-up, hoovering, shopping, and decorating) and he sometimes does the main meal. He does it because 'I've nothing else to do and its nice to see a clean tidy house, but there's no financial reward', though there are three tasks he will not do; windows, ironing, and washing. Most unusually the three managerial tasks of planning the meals, making the shopping list and household budgeting are now all shared in the Bradshaw household. Mr Bradshaw also helps his wife with her job, taking out all the rubbish and getting up for difficult male residents in the night. Again he regrets that this is unpaid. It is worth adding that Mrs Bradshaw earns just enough for her husband to be unable to claim any state benefit at all.

She loves her job – 'we should do more for our older people' – and though she knows 'it doesn't pay me to work, he worked for me and the kids so why can't I work for him? I wouldn't like to have social workers in'. But the job is demanding, 'and that's why I need Malcolm around to depend on'. Mrs Bradshaw is most appreciative of what her husband does for her, but sees it as very difficult for him to adapt to his new role: 'It doesn't matter to me if I work or not. It's more important for men. It's been inbred into them'. Mr Bradshaw now bears a substantial domestic burden, but for him it is no substitute for being the breadwinner and though he is pleased that 'we're both independent of the state, at the end of the day we're pounds out of pocket'. It is obvious that Mr Bradshaw would dearly love financial recognition for his role in the house, and for the help he gives his wife in her job.

Chapter 5

Motivations and household work strategies: gender, conflict, and the family

Substitution between the formal and complementary economies in the context of recession

Whilst the last chapter has examined the changes in gender relations that take place within the domestic economy when men become unemployed, the present one is concerned with the effects of these changes, which can be seen on two different planes: the economic and the personal. These are covered in the first two sections of the chapter respectively. First, there is the effect of changing work strategies within the domestic sector on the complementary and the formal economies. This section provides empirical material to add to the typology suggested in the first chapter and examines the gender effects of change. Second, there is the effect of changing family work strategies – whether in the complementary or the formal economy – on the family itself and the individuals within it. This adjustment process will differ between women and men, depending on external circumstances on the one hand, and on attitudes to roles on the other. The third section of the chapter takes an overview of family work strategies, examining the conflicting motivations at work for different family members. It also considers the role that the state plays in perpetuating traditional gender ideologies.

In the final section, links are made between the economic and the personal themes, which interrelate with one another and raise important questions for economic theory. On the one hand, economic realities affect individual behaviour; on the other, the behaviour of individuals influences economic variables. Economic theory makes assumptions about how individuals behave: as 'rational economic men' (*sic*). The concluding section shows that such an assumption is an erroneous simplification. What is required for a more realistic economic model of individual behaviour, is an awareness of the different and conflicting motivations that operate for men and women, who make economic and personal decisions, not as individuals, but as members of a family. A new model for negotiations over the gender division of household work is finally suggested.

At a society-wide level, unemployment leads to a change in the distribution of wealth and opportunity. At an individual level, when a member of a family becomes unemployed, and leaves the labour market, they are likely to suffer a drop in income, but the other major change is in time available. Economic theory would predict that this should bring about the possibility of a series of substitutions. First, more extra self-consumption activities might be undertaken within the domestic sector to replace the purchase of goods or services which have become too expensive to buy in the formal economy. Second, more use might be made of the voluntary economy, since this again is a less expensive source for families on a lower income. Finally, the unemployed might replace employment in the formal economy with employment in the irregular sector, or they might become purchasers of cheaper goods and services from that economy. Each of these substitutions relies on a re-allocation of the unemployed person's time, so that work activity is transferred from one sector to another. It is important to remember, however, that even in the domestic or the voluntary sector, work may require more than simply labour power. It may need capital equipment, materials or skills, and the unemployed may be lacking in any one of these.

Looking first at extra self-consumption activities, the households in the sample did not appear to have taken on many additional activities in this category. Rather over half the wives and a third of the husbands did work in the household which could alternatively be provided through the market. For most of the women this was knitting or baking, but men's work was more varied, ranging from extensive decorating and DIY to repairing the car, fixing electrical appliances and putting in a new bathroom suite. The nature of the tasks undertaken indicated a traditional gender division of labour, but the extent of extra self-consumption activity appeared comparable between spouses. The extra self-provisioning done by husbands often related to the man's former employment, so that for example two of the men who undertook domestic electrical repairs were electricians by trade, and there was also a fitter and a former motor mechanic who undertook related extra self-consumption activities.

It may be remembered from Setting the scene 1, however, that many of the sample men had employment skills that could not be readily translated to the domestic economy, and only one man had attended a course – in motor mechanics – explicitly to acquire such a skill. This last case fits in well with economic theory of the opportunity cost of time: his wife was a self-employed hairdresser on low earnings, who used an older car for her work, which her husband could then service. It is interesting that one family had been anticipating the husband's redundancy for some time – a fitter with the Coal Board – and had recently sold their automatic washing machine to replace it with a single tub machine, on the grounds that he would be able to fix it if it went wrong.

Whilst there was, then, an appreciable level of additional domestic economy activity in the sample, it was by no means at the level that a recent article in *The Economist* (1987) sees as possible. This suggested that the opportunities for substituting household spending in the formal economy with work at home were high for nearly 19 per cent of household spending, medium to low for nearly 39 per cent and nil for some 42 per cent. How far did the sample families have the necessary equipment and materials to replace market purchases with domestic economy activities? At a fairly basic level, nearly two-thirds of the households had electric drills, but of course it is not much use being able to repair the family car if the family cannot afford to run a car in the first place. Not surprisingly in view of their low incomes, only a dozen of the thirty families had cars which belonged to parents rather than children. In three families the parents used push-bikes.

This provides an example of disinvestment in consumer durables in unemployed households. However, there are contradictory pressures with regard to the cost of materials: whilst one family commented that they did not have enough money to decorate, in another family the husband's redundancy pay was being used to finance extensive decorating, DIY, and home improvements. A final factor influencing the extent of home improvement work in the domestic sector was that only one third of the sample were owner occupiers. Pahl (1984), for example, has shown that DIY spending is higher for home owners, and sees the high incidence of owner-occupation on Sheppey, where he undertook his empirical work, as one of the factors making for high levels of self-provisioning there.

Turning now to the voluntary sector, this is not much used as a cost saver, as economic theory might suggest, but rather as a time absorber. Most of this work was done by households containing unemployed men for others. A certain amount was done on an exchange basis, but very little voluntary economy work flowed inwards. It is worth distinguishing the voluntary economy work involving relatives from that involving neighbours, friends, or others. Nearly half the husbands, and just over half the wives, were undertaking tasks for relatives. Most of the men who undertook additional self-provisioning activities inside the household did male gendered tasks for relatives, but a similar number of men also undertook the more conventionally female 'caring' tasks. Men's caring tasks included looking after grandchildren, and in one case taking them to school every day, visiting elderly parents, or getting shopping for them.

A characteristic of caring tasks is that they do not require capital equipment or materials, and the fact that husbands were undertaking this kind of work indicates that men are prepared to develop their skills in a caring direction. Wives also undertook caring tasks, as well as decorating, icing cakes, and doing buffets. It was noticeable that our families were doing far more for their relatives than the other way round. Whilst in one family there was a two-way flow of voluntary sector work between the relatives, only two families had an explicit exchange in kind with relatives. Thus, one husband did electrical repairs in exchange for home brew, whilst his wife did buffets for the family and her brother laid out their garden and did her 'real decorating'. These families were insistent that no money changed hands.

There were fewer families who did work for neighbours, friends, or others, but still over half the households were involved. Here, rather more husbands than wives were undertaking similar sorts of tasks to those done for relatives. For example, one man visited a neighbour three times a week in hospital, and helped elderly ladies living nearby with small repairs; while another paid the rent for several neighbours. Again more work was done for others than for our families, but a new feature was that a few tasks were paid for. In two families the cases of payment involved fostering: this is obviously not part of the irregular sector, and indeed the fostering allowance might well be considered simply as expenses. One husband, who was on invalidity benefit, was paid for undertaking the secretarial duties of his local working men's club, but did not earn over the higher earnings limit applicable. Unfortunately it was not clear whether the former fisherman got paid in cash or in kind for the occasional net-mending that he did: this was the only possible case of involvement in the irregular economy in the sample. It is finally worth mentioning that in nearly a third of the families, children were involved in the voluntary sector. For example one 12-year-old girl stayed overnight with a recently divorced neighbour to keep her company, and an 18-year-old daughter had gone to live with her widowed grandmother for the same reason.

The irregular sector then, was noticeable in its absence from the sample, at least in terms of working within it, since the net-mending was the only possible case. There was thus no disguised unemployment in the families interviewed. Unfortunately families were not asked whether they made purchases in the irregular economy, which was one of the methods used in the American study by Ferman and Berndt (1981). There are a number of possible reasons why there was so little irregular work in the sample. It has already been suggested that there are skills and capital equipment limitations on how far men can work in the voluntary and domestic sectors; the same limitations operate in the irregular sector. A second factor is that wives were working, so that these were not unemployed households with no wage income coming in, and the need to supplement state benefits was therefore less important as a pressure. Finally, there is the high potential danger of working and claiming, which several respondents commented on.

Taking both the voluntary sector and the additional self-consumption activities performed by families over and above the housework and family care performed within each household, it can be concluded that there was an extensive involvement in the social economy amongst the sample families, particularly with respect to relatives, but also with other outsiders. Pahl and Wallace (in Redclift and Mingione 1985:218) talk of a process of polarisation between busy households with many workers who are employed, do domestic tasks, own homes and cars, and have money to maintain them, and unemployed households. In contrast, despite the men being out of work in the Wearside sample, families were participating in the social economy to a considerable extent. Where wives do work, even for low wages, and despite the deterrent effect of benefit regulations, it would seem that families are able to avoid some of the most debilitating features of the unemployed household. The evidence also points to a lack of gender differentiation in this involvement, although there was some gender division in the type of work done. Again, this indicates some differences with Pahl's opinion that 'women are perhaps more likely to perceive the household as the basic economic unit and to arrange their balance of work in terms of the needs of the household as a whole' (Pahl 1984:85). Indeed, the fact that husbands were becoming involved in the social economy at all is contrary to the evidence of social policy researchers, who have found that it is generally middle-class women who undertake this sort of work. Taking their involvement in the social economy together with the gender shift in housework and childcare observed in the previous chapter, it would seem that men on Wearside who have no employment are showing themselves to be highly flexible, and are being responsive to a total household work strategy within which their wives have taken on paid work. The next section will look at how far these shifts in work strategies provide men with a means of coping with unemployment.

Personal effects: strategies for coping with unemployment

It is possible – though undoubtedly difficult – to gain an identity from unpaid, 'non-work' as well as from paid work or employment. As feminists have pointed out, the very terms used make for difficulty: 'The modern concept of work, as the expenditure of energy for financial gain, defines housework as the most inferior and marginal work of all' (Oakley 1976:4). This study has been concerned with the gender interaction between three sorts of work – in the domestic economy, in the voluntary economy, and in the formal one, with only the last as paid – and has considered it important to look at all three types of work to get a picture of an individual family's work profile or strategy. The men in the sample have been excluded from the world of paid work; to what extent have they been able to develop an identity from the other forms of work? Feminists have been very concerned with the difficulties for women of having an identity which is linked to domestic work, which leads many women to see themselves as 'just a housewife'.

> Housework differs from most other work in three significant ways: it is private, is is self-defined and its outlines are blurred by its integration in a whole complex of domestic, family-based roles, which define the situation of women as well as the situation of housewife.

> (Oakley 1976:6)

Given that men's roles are traditionally strongly linked with bread-winning in the world of paid work and in the public domain, how are men adjusting to being at home? As Tolson points out 'As individuals, men are brought up to value work as an end in itself, and to fix their personal identities around particular occupations' (Tolson 1977:13). It is important to realise that what can be said of the sample families with respect to adjustment is inevitably sketchy and impressionistic, for 'definitions of gender enter into some of the basic meanings attached to work, leisure, family life' (ibid.:17). It is nevertheless possible to make a provisional assessment of how men are adjusting to what is effectively a shift from the public domain, normally associated with male roles, to the private domain, usually associated with female ones. With unemployment the 'domestic workplace' becomes accentuated as the location for social life and interaction.

We have already seen that, at its simplest, becoming unemployed involves two important changes: loss of income, and an increase of time available, so that an unemployed person will have 40 additional hours of 'unobligated' time, time in which they are not required at work. On average, people spend 45 hours a week sleeping, 31 hours on personal care, eating meals, etc., 29 hours in paid employment and an estimated 2 hours in the irregular sector, leaving 61 hours of 'discretionary' time for work in the domestic sector and for leisure (Rose 1983). One way to examine the effects of unemployment is to compare the use of time between employed and unemployed individuals. Trew and Kilpatrick (1984) use a combination of activity check lists and time-budgets in the form of diaries, to achieve this, in a study in Northern Ireland. This enables them to look at the life styles of the unemployed, and to classify them according to clusters of activities into four groups. An 'active' cluster spends more time on active, participatory leisure and work-related activities, such as looking for work, whilst a 'social' cluster devotes more time to social life and travelling to reach it. A 'domestic' cluster use more time on domestic chores, whilst a 'passive' cluster spends a large part of the day on passive leisure, such as watching television, spending more of their time with their family, and more time on childcare.

An alternative approach to studying the effects of unemployment is that of Ian Miles (1983), who is particularly concerned with its psychological dimensions. Basing his methodology on the work of Jahoda (1982), his hypothesis is that unemployed people with greater access to five 'categories of experience' (ACE) will display less of the psychological debilitation associated with unemployment. Jahoda, in her classic overview of the social and psychological effects of unemployment, points out that a job has latent functions as well as financial rewards. Employment fulfills five categories of experience to which the unemployed have limited access. In the first place, paid work enforces activity. Second, such activity takes the form of a habitual time structure for the working day, so that the time experience of the unemployed should not be regarded as leisure, since leisure is a complement to working hours, not a substitute for them. In addition employment provides social contacts, as well as a sense of collective or social purpose. Finally, work confers social status and identity on the employee. Jahoda sums this up in terms of employment providing an opportunity to test reality.

Such a framework allows a preliminary assessment of unemployment as a source of conflict within the family to be made, before undertaking a critique of the models for negotiations over the gender division of household work strategies in the next section. Unlike the work of Trew and Kilpatrick and of Miles, my own study pinpoints the gender dimensions of the effects of male unemployment. My work also supplements the conclusions they reach, particularly with respect to the process of adjustment, and to attitudes of husbands and wives to any gender changes in household work strategies resulting from male unemployment. The general parameters within which I examined men's adjustment to no longer being in paid work was in terms of objective and subjective factors. In outline, the objective factors involve an assessment of what the men in the sample did in place of their 40 hours per week involvement in the labour market. There are four alternatives here, two of which have already been looked at: involvement in the domestic sector and in the voluntary sector. If we combine these two with a consideration of leisure activities and the search for jobs, we can compare the extent to which men have created either a home-based or a non home-based lifestyle for themselves. Taking a look at subjective factors, men's attitudes to doing housework in particular may conflict with their practice, thus limiting the practical adjustment process.

It is possible that conflict in either attitudes or practice between spouses may impede the husband's adjustment to not being in paid work. On the other hand a joint sharing attitude to work in the domestic economy may allow for a home-based adjustment which is underpinned by the development of an alternative joint life style with his wife. What the rest of this section does then, is to make a provisional overall assessment of the extent to which the men in the sample have adjusted to a very major change in their lives: the change from full-time work to non-employment. Broad divisions are made between those who can be seen as 'adjusted' to the change in some sense, those who are 'semi-adjusted', and those who are 'non-adjusted'. It is important to realise that these divisions are very much provisional ones, for they are based on a snapshot view of the family obtained in one interview. A range of variables made up the overall combination, many of which directly concern the extent to which men have created alternatives to work.

First, then, was the amount of housework and childcare that men undertook, though this had, second, to be balanced by individual attitudes to undertaking such work. Third, there was the level of involvement in the social economy, as well as in leisure activities and hobbies. Fifth, was the development of a joint lifestyle with his wife. Men's attitudes to not being in paid work and the extent of their job search, together with their feelings about job prospects were also important. These variables also provide an overview of a home-based or a traditional, non-home-based, direction to the adjustment process. Finally the presence of appreciable conflicts between husband and wife – or its obverse, a sensitivity to each other's needs – will also affect the process, but it is the combination of objective and subjective factors which determines the outcome.

Let us start by looking at attitudes to housework on the part of men and women. It is possible to distinguish five broad types, remembering that of course husbands and wives may hold different attitudes. First, there were those who feel that housework should be shared between men and women. Typical comments by husbands here were that it would be 'more loving if men did more'; or that 'it's a good thing now. Times have changed. It was always women's work. They should both share'. Second, there were those who felt that men should help or participate in housework. Such an attitude was expressed by husbands in terms of 'All men should help. You don't realise how lonely housewives can be' or 'I don't see anything wrong with it, but not a frilly pinny or a feather duster'; or by wives as 'I don't mind him doing it. But sometimes I know he's sick of the roles being reversed', or, 'I think all men should help in the house'. Third amongst the more common attitudes were those who hold traditional or patriarchal views. As two husbands from exchanged-roles families put it: 'Very belittling really. A man shouldn't do the housework. I'll do it, that's it', and 'I believe in the man working and the woman being in the house'. Some wives' comments included, 'Why I don't really like it you know, but with me going out to work it's a big help'. For a small number of people it may be the time dimension that determines attitudes: 'it kills the boredom' or 'it occupies my mind'. Or it may be the power or authority that wives gain from their work: 'I cannot expect the wife to come in and do it after a full day's work', or, 'well, if he didn't do it, it wouldn't get done'.

Men's abstract views on doing housework can be further expanded by considering the reasons they give for doing, or not doing, housework. It was noticeable that the majority of husbands gave reasons for doing housework in terms of the amount of time they had available: 'It's better than staring at the TV', 'it keeps us on the go: I'm still up at seven', or, more positively, of wanting to help or share with their wives. Substantially fewer said that they got satisfaction from it, but a number also saw domestic work as some sort of necessity; typical comments would be: 'I'm not just a passenger' or 'I'm not going to neglect me bairns'. The reasons for not doing housework were often couched in terms of an unwillingness to do specific tasks on the part of the husband, or indeed the wife expressing reservations about him taking on certain tasks. These are 'male-based rationales', which argue that women are better or more skilled at doing certain tasks than men.

There was an interesting gender difference in the specific housework and childcare tasks that men and women said they liked best and least. It was noticeable that women were more specific than men about which housework tasks they liked, and particularly which they disliked, while men were more inclined to be non-specific. The more precise expression of women's likes and dislikes probably reflects the fact that they actually do more housework than men, and of course it has already been argued that even in exchanged-role households women still undertake a core of housework and childcare tasks. In contrast, it was women who were less specific about childcare tasks, with nearly half the wives replying that they liked everything about bringing children up. This would seem to accord well with the centrality of the motherhood role for the sample women both in practice and in theory: it was a role that was on the one hand genuinely enjoyed; on the other, not questioned. Again though, the gender differences between what is liked and disliked tend to indicate that the women had day to day duties, whilst men were more involved in special occasions such as taking their children out.

What, then, can be said about how far attitudes to who should do the housework coincide with who actually does it? In the majority of families with traditional rigid, traditional flexible, and sharing forms of organisation there was a reasonable approximation between 'theory' and 'practice', to use some convenient shorthand terms. In other words, there was a broad correspondence between traditional or patriarchal attitudes and traditional rigid practice, between helping or participating – what might be called 'modified traditional' – attitudes and traditional flexible practice, and between sharing attitudes and practice. However, in Setting the scene for this chapter, two case studies have been taken which indicate that in some families practice is noticeably less traditional and gender segregated than views on roles. Four families in the sample had such a marked discrepancy between theory and practice that they were placed in a sub-category of 'reluctant'. There were two reluctant traditional flexible families, and for one wife in this category, even a small contribution from her husband was a problem for her: 'It's degrading. He's a man and a man should be out working, not doing the housework. I've nothing against him doing it, but I've always done it. It's my role.' There were also two reluctant sharers, who either had no ideology of sharing, or a strongly traditional ideology. There was a sense in which change had been forced upon them, involving resentment of their household organisation. It was noticeable that in reluctant families it was particularly the wife's attitudes that were more traditional than the practice.

In exchanged-role households too, attitudes to roles seemed generally to lag behind, and in some cases far behind, the non-traditional practice of these families. Those families who had moved from a traditional flexible organisation before the husband lost his job, usually had fairly sharing attitudes, but this certainly did not go as far as approving of exchanged roles, as can be seen in the case of the Bradshaws in Setting the scene. In families who were traditional rigid before, there was not even a helping attitude present beforehand for the men concerned. Whilst in reluctant families, it was the wives whose views tended to be more traditional, a general feature of exchanged-role families was that it was their wives' working that had forced men into a domestic role, so that it was particularly men's attitudes and practice that could be quite seriously out of line with each other.

In sum then, views of who should do what in the way of housework and childcare, and the practice of who actually does what broadly coincide; with the exception of the reluctant category within shared or traditional flexible families and in exchanged-role families. In these cases, practice tended to be less traditional than perceptions of roles, particularly for women in the former group and for men in the latter. I am not trying to suggest a total lack of conflict between theory and practice, or indeed between spouses, over who should do the housework; simply that a general overall correspondence made conflict muted and low key in the majority of cases. It could be added that in traditional flexible families it would appear that to some extent practice – perhaps induced by the husband's boredom – led attitudes.

In sharing households, men no longer being in paid work had, in contrast, sometimes allowed sharing attitudes to housework and childcare to be put into practice. In the minority of households however, there was conflict between views and practice, a factor which made for tension within the household on the one hand; and made it more difficult for men, and their wives, to adjust to unemployment on the other. Conflict between men and women over standards and routines is of course implicit in bottoming, where in the less traditionally organised households, wives were still taking responsibility for thorough cleaning, often at weekends, despite the fact that their husbands may be doing the cleaning as part of their routine through the week.

It is also important to make an objective assessment of the extent to which men have been able to replace the time formerly spent in paid work with other activities and to judge the extent to which husbands have created an alternative life style for themselves. By considering men's involvement in the domestic and the voluntary economy, their leisure and hobby activities, and whether they have developed a strong joint lifestyle with their wife or not, it is possible to distinguish between home based and traditional or non home-based alternatives. Since half the families had non-traditional, exchanged-role, and sharing forms of household organisation, and under a quarter were traditional rigid, it is not surprising to find that the majority of men fall into the home-based category, especially given the level of involvement of men in the social economy discussed in the previous section.

A brief look at two typical families will help to clarify the distinction. Mr Turner had chosen the home-based alternative. In the first place, he does a substantial amount of housework and childcare in an exchanged-role household. It is true that he works in the voluntary economy outside the home, helping relatives with their cars and doing odd electrical repairs for neighbours; but he also undertakes extra self-consumption activities within the home, repairing the caravette and domestic appliances. But his leisure activities are very much with his wife and family, going camping twice a month and other outings. He and his wife are also foster parents. 'I now have every weekend free with the family, unlike being on shifts'. As Trew and Kilpatrick (1984) comment of their 'domestic cluster' there are similarities between the life of those men who have opted for the home based alternative and the housewife. In addition, for the spouses concerned, their life styles have become more gender congruent and less gender specific.

Mr Bewick's activities however are clearly non home-based. He is from a traditional flexible household, and does only a limited amount of housework, whilst his children are adult. His work in the voluntary economy involved going outside the immediate household to help his mother. His leisure activities are clearly non home-based since he goes out to his clubs regularly twice a day.

> Two clubs I keep in touch with . . . since leaving work I find that a full day without mixing with other male grown ups makes it a long, boring, tiring day . . . . I more or less *insist* on that . . . it's a break talking to others. I'm out with other men.

This involves the traditional, gender segregated, model.

The home-based, gender congruent alternative may also be supplemented by spouses creating what can be called an 'alternative joint lifestyle' for themselves. I have already indicated several families in which there was a strong attitude from both husband and wife that household and childcare tasks should be shared and where there seemed to be sensitivity to each other's needs. Families in the sharing category – with the exception of those in the reluctant group – have all developed such a joint life style. There are also some families in the traditional flexible group who are like this, but one would not expect to find it amongst traditional rigid families. It also tends not to be present in exchanged-role families since the wife works too long hours to be able to share very much with her husband. The Bradshaws described in Setting the scene at the start of this chapter are an exception here, but it will be remembered on the one hand that Mrs Bradshaw works from home, and on the other that her husband helps her with that work. This alternative joint life style, signs of which are present in at least half the sample, probably has some similarities with the life style some couples adopt when they retire.

It is possible to make some overall comments on the nature of leisure activities and pastimes for the men in the sample. Amongst most these were limited in their extent, so that for example one husband claimed that his leisure activities only involved looking after his fish, though he actually had quite a sophisticated pond in the garden for them. Looking more closely at the nature of leisure activities and pastimes, these can be distinguished by the former involving expenditure in the formal economy. For many of the unemployed, income limitations restrict the use of their additional discretionary time on leisure consumption. It is therefore not surprising that social leisure activities might only involve going to the club or for a drink once or twice a week, and that the cheapest form of passive leisure consumption, watching TV or videos, should play an important part in many men's leisure consumption patterns. This emphasises the complementary nature of employment and leisure consumption and the problems of substituting the latter for the former.

Involvement in pastimes throws up different issues: the limited extent of these can perhaps be explained by the heavy manual labour and the overtime that many of these men had experienced whilst in paid work. This meant that they had not developed the contacts and skills necessary for active involvement in pastimes whilst employed. It must of course also be remembered that some of the men had a relatively high involvement in the domestic and voluntary economies, which used up a part of their discretionary time. It is nevertheless noticeable that only three of the men stood out in terms of the absorbing nature of their pastimes. One of these painted oils, drew cartoons, went to a local art club, and spent a good deal of time in the reference library, whilst another went hill walking and rambling, was on the rambling club committee and was writing a detailed diary of all his walks.

What then do men, and their wives, feel about no longer being in work; for this is the other side of the coin to men being at home? The generally negative attitudes to men not being in paid work was underlined by the fact that only one family expressed a positive preference for it; though wives had more positive things to say about it than husbands, and appreciated the advantages to family life of their husbands no longer working. Men and women both disliked the lack of money involved when men were not working. It was noticeable however that the most disliked thing for men was boredom or the fact that they had too much time; while for women various aspects of the conflicts that arose in the home were important: arguments, getting on each other's nerves, the household routine spoiled. Men found that not being in work affected their status: it was belittling, they felt on the scrap heap, they lacked purpose; and they also missed the companionship of work. A few of both women and men alluded to the depression arising from unemployment.

Men's dislike of unemployment did not on the whole stand in contrast to a love of work; for the majority of men, work was very much seen as a means to the end of earning a living for the family. 'It was a job at the time' as one man put it, or another: 'there's nobody gangs out to work for fun'. Nevertheless, finding themselves out of work was a traumatic experience for some: 'when you've worked for thirty odd years and then you're on the heap'. Those seeking work were noticeably pessimistic over the prospects of obtaining it. One husband aged 47 felt fine when he first became unemployed; that is, until his first interview at the job centre, when he was asked how old he was: 'I felt terrible then – I've never looked at myself as old. I think it's the biggest shock in the world, knowing that I'll never get work again unless I'm really lucky'. It appeared, then, that there was strong attachment to the role of breadwinner for many of the men in the sample.

Wives were of course working whilst their husbands were unemployed; what were their attitudes to their own paid work? It has already been suggested in Setting the scene 1 that both the hours that the sample women worked and the length of time they had been in their current job indicated a substantial commitment to the labour market, and indeed three women had worked throughout their married lives. There were a number of women who discussed their jobs in considerable detail and with obvious enthusiasm during the interview, and this comes across from some of the case studies in Setting the scene 2. Many of the sample women had an obvious pride in their work, and several husbands volunteered that their wives really enjoyed their work. It was striking that what women liked about their jobs was the opportunity for caring for people and communicating with them: precisely what is seen as characteristic of much of 'women's work'. On the whole, dislikes were expressed in a distinctly low key, and only three women expressed serious reservations about their job.

Husband's attitudes to the general issue of mothers working were varied, with some holding to the view that men should be bread-winners, but equally an awareness of the financial necessity for women to work, and with a concern for the needs of children and of wives. When it came to the practical issue of what they felt about their own wife working, there was a noticeable adaptability to practical exigencies. Only one man felt his wife should not have been working, and it is not surprising that his wife had since given up her job. Often husbands expressed the positive benefits of wives working: 'She's got a decent headpiece on her. She's used to working and having her independence. She'd just go stale doing housework all the time'. A number of husbands were also grateful that their wives were earning, something that may in part be a recognition of the relative increase in her economic power.

Having taken a closer look at some of the variables which determine whether it is possible to develop an identity from 'non-work' as well as from 'work' it is now time to ask to what extent and in what ways the men in the sample had been able to build any such alternative identity. How can men adjust to being home based, and what mechanisms can they use to cope? When there is a core of attachment to traditional roles, what one is inevitably talking about here is a *level* of adaptation, a *level* of adjustment. There is bound to be conflict over roles and identity in the face of adjustment, but to what extent can men get away from a one-sided emphasis on employment as the only significant form of work or activity? Within the three main categories of adjusted, semi-adjusted, and unadjusted, are a range of sub-categories which can best be explained in terms of some comparisons which clarify their predominant characteristics. Within the adjusted category can be found those who are adjusted to poor job prospects, those who have opted for a traditional, gender segregated, adjustment; and two sorts of home-based adjustment, one based on exchanging roles, the other based on sharing.

Amongst the unadjusted are those who are desperate for a job, those who have not adjusted to the home base, and an 'unadjusted status' group who have failed to provide themselves with an alternative identity for a variety of reasons.

In the case of traditional adjustment, men do not take on any housework or childcare tasks as a response to unemployment, and this is reflected in a traditional rigid form of household organisation. The wife may have some minor complaints about her husband not contributing, but essentially she is happy that he should have leisure activities which take him outside the house: 'he's better when he's out'. Husbands will develop traditional male activities as a substitute for work, whether they be social activities, such as going to the club or the betting shop, or involvement in male gendered activities in the social economy, or extra domestic self-consumption activities such as mending cars. Wives will either be working relatively low hours, or may well have given up their employment since their husband lost his job. Whilst there is no development of a joint life style within this group, there is not any major conflict between husbands and wives, and each agrees to maintain their gender segregated roles. Husbands will be looking for work, but will tend to see it as unlikely to yield a job in the present climate. In terms of Jahoda's (1982) access to categories of experience, it is involvement in a male gendered social life and work in the voluntary sector that provides social contacts and an habitual, albeit limited, time structure to the day. Social status and identity are maintained by a nurturing of traditional attitudes to gender roles within the family.

In contrast a home-based adjustment process involves a movement towards less gender differentiation in a variety of ways. The first type here is a sharing-based adjustment, where the men concerned all contribute to housework and childcare in a sharing household organisation. This is combined with a reasonably positive attitude towards housework by the men concerned; but perhaps more importantly, there is a strong sharing attitude between husband and wife. Wives tend to be working an intermediate number of hours. Husbands in this group often have strongly developed leisure activities outside the home, but this tends to confirm that they are making use of their non-employment time rather than any traditional orientation. None of these men is seeking work very vigorously for a variety of reasons: for instance, one man is currently enjoying the opportunities that not being in work are providing him. In terms of access to categories of experience, both the time structure and the social contacts of this group of unemployed tend to be gender-congruent. The sense of collective or social purpose is maintained through involvement in the family and domestic arena, in a manner which one might expect of couples who have opted to job share or perhaps of some retired couples.

141

Those who have adjusted to exchanged roles are slightly different. Men who fall into this category are fairly fully occupied within the domestic sector by household and childcare tasks, but they also work a good deal in the voluntary sector and seem to have leisure activities which occupy much of what remains of their time. However, these men have traditional views of roles, so that their domestic work role is not without conflict: 'You know I've always believed it's a man's place to work. I think married women shouldn't work.' Yet in these families, the wives have made a firm decision to work full-time, given the poor prospects for their husbands. Albeit without enormous enthusiasm, the men in this category have taken on a large share of domestic responsibility and have probably established some identity from this role. Their lives are similar to those of a full-time housewife, and the process of adjustment is the most gender congruent.

There is, thirdly, an adjustment which is based on a realistic assessment of poor job prospects. It can be seen as a non-domestic adjustment in that although the men in this group make some contribution to the domestic sector within a traditional flexible household organisation, it is not very substantial. Neither is their contribution to the voluntary sector very large. Whilst they are looking for work, they accept that the prospects are poor. This group has limited access to the categories of experience of Jahoda (1982), and might be seen as approximating to a retired life style, with some involvement in passive pastimes, such as doing puzzle books or reading extensively, or development of an alternative life style with their wife. This category of adjustment appears as objectively the least secure, and has some similarities with the semi-adjusted. The main feature of the semi-adjusted group is that there is some conflict between husband and wife, which means that the men concerned have only been able to make a partial adjustment to the home base. These households tend to be traditional flexible ones, with modified traditional views of roles and where wives are usually working over 16 hours a week. It is noticeable that two of these families fall in the reluctant category, and the conflict present makes it difficult for husbands to maintain a sense of social purpose.

Those who are unadjusted to their home base, lack access to all the major categories of experience that would be available to them were they employed. This group has either a traditional flexible or a traditional rigid form of household organisation, so that men are not much involved in the domestic economy, neither do they turn outside the home for activity. These men are not involved in the social economy in any way, and their limited leisure activities – crosswords and TV or reading the papers – do not seem to fill their time. They have not much hope of obtaining employment, and there is considerable conflict between husband and wife.

The key to understanding the final two categories of men who have not adjusted relates to their lack of social status and identity in the face of job loss. For one of these groups the lack of status is primarily explicable from the effects of the social security system. For the other it is the lack of a job itself. Within the category of those desperate for a job there are big variations in the contribution to the domestic economy, but each makes a contribution to the social economy, and has some fairly limited leisure activities. A key feature of this group is that they appear to be quite heavily depressed; one husband for example had lost weight and now weighs less than 9 stones. It was very difficult to arrange interviews with these families, and it was apparent from the doorstep interview described in Setting the scene 1, that unwillingness to be interviewed was related to the depression arising from not working. Another indicator of how much these men would like to work is that they have taken short-term jobs despite the problems this causes in sorting out benefits. It is also noticeable that these men would be prepared to 'do anything and work for anything' as one wife put it.

Amongst the former group, lacking in social status because of the social security system, there is also a desperate desire for a job: these men have strong work ethics, and very traditional views of roles. Whilst some of them make a substantial contribution to the domestic sector, they do not have any attachment to it. None of them has enough leisure activities to occupy themselves, and so they are bored. However, in addition to wanting employment, these men feel that the social security system has been unjust to them, as is apparent for both Mr Bradshaw and Mr Giles from Setting the scene at the start of the chapter.

In conclusion, then, it can be argued that the flexibility and adaptability shown by the men in the sample were primarily based on a pragmatic response to practical circumstances. In general it was practical circumstances that lead to change rather than abstract attitudes to roles. Nevertheless there could be serious conflict between traditional, patriarchal attitudes, and practice; in which case the gender division of labour actually adopted within the household tended to be more liberal than attitudes. In other words, the complexities of adjustment and adaptation appear to be primarily practically based. It may be cautiously, and it may be unwillingly, but amongst Wearside men who have lost their jobs and whose wives are working, are men who are taking on new roles which by no means correspond to traditional stereotypes.

It is nevertheless important to be clear that any 'adjustment' to non-employment is very much a second-best path: these men would clearly far rather be in paid work. In this respect, I would very much agree with the reservations that Trew and Kilpatrick expressed in their work: 'Most of the unemployed men . . . . had imposed a pattern on their lives, some having developed a life style which they found satisfactory, but few ... lived lives which compensated for their lack of employment' (1984:45). The difficulties of adjustment can be explained in terms of the lack of access to Jahoda's (1982) five categories of experience generally enjoyed by those in employment, so that as Miles says, 'It would be unwise to see these patterns of time use as reflecting constructive coping strategies, the grateful seizing of opportunities for personal development' (1983:50).

What I have also been able to show, is the way in which the gender division of work both within and outside the household can be re-negotiated in response to male unemployment. The next section will consider more fully the way in which this can give rise to conflict within the household. Meanwhile, it is important to be aware that it is in the nature of the sample chosen – with wives in employment – that numbers should be skewed towards home based adjustment and away from the unadjusted category. In addition, although the response rate was high, self-selection by families would tend to exclude those where adjustment was a problem. My research indicates the types of adjustment and non-adjustment that men may experience, rather than the proportions in each category.

Economic restructuring: the family and conflicting motivations

In this section, consideration will be given to the way in which the material pressures of unemployment towards a less rigid division of labour in household work strategies are counteracted by the role of the state in perpetuating traditional ideologies amongst the sample families. As the last section has suggested, more traditional ideological beliefs within the family were in any case often at variance with practice. Chapter 3 has already looked at the issue of ideology in relation to women undertaking paid work, but it is worth focusing for a moment on ideology and housework. Both the origins and the persistence of house-work being seen as women's work can be linked with the role of ideology. While Hartmann (1979) argues that the material basis for patriarchy rests most fundamentally in men's control over women's labour power, in terms of access to jobs and restricting women's sexuality, Pauline Hunt (1978) identifies three related ideologies which buttress men's power.

First, men are seen as breadwinners, second, women are seen as homemakers, and third, wages are seen as a payment for individual work, whilst all three ideologies are firmly rooted in prevailing social practice. Thus the occupation of houseworker is an all-embracing status, with no separation of function: wifehood and work are inextricably joined. For the man on the other hand, the separation of wage work from domestic work has the effect of releasing the male wage worker almost completely from responsibilities at home. Indeed the second, woman's income is usually regarded by the family as a windfall, reinforcing the ideology of the women as a homemaker. Husbands, however, need to bring in a 'family wage'.

Yet in many respects, material circumstances do much to contradict what Barrett and McIntosh argue is the myth of the family wage. The structure of the family and of the labour market are actually independent of each other, so that 'many male wage-earners do not have dependents and many of the unwaged members of the working class do not have breadwinners' (Barrett and McIntosh 1980:57). In fact the wages of 'heads of household' only contribute 51 per cent to household income; the rest comes from state benefits, self-employment, the employment of wives (making up 11.4 per cent), and of other household members (10.8 per cent). Now of course, the Wearside families studied, were in circumstances which negated much of the basis for a patriarchal attitude: none of the husbands was in employment, and unemployment makes a nonsense of ideas of a male breadwinner and a family wage. Indeed, particularly wives in full-time employment, were often regarded as the breadwinner, whilst, as we have seen, a substantial proportion of husbands was taking on more domestic work than previously. Negotiations over the gender division of labour within and outside the household were thus subject to a conflict between the traditional, or patriarchal model, and the rationality, or maximisation of economic interests model, which has already been discussed in Chapter 3.

There are two ways in which the state exacerbates this possibility for conflict within the family. First, there is the gender bias in the benefits system which derives from the assumptions underlying the Beveridge system, and which, as we have seen in Chapter 2, no longer correspond to the structural realities of the British economy. Thus, paid employment no longer prevents financial poverty. Female heads of household in particular are likely to be low paid; full-time work is no longer the norm, again predominately for women; full employment for men is proving no longer feasible, particularly in the regions; and finally, married women who undertake paid employment are no longer appropriately regarded as financial appendages of their husbands or co-habitees. The new income support system does not radically alter this situation: it is essentially designed to reduce the costs of the welfare system. The second exacerbation is through state-structured low pay.

It is interesting to pause for a moment to consider how both the social security system and low pay interact with the market system. Ostensibly, in furnishing a system of welfare support, the state is insulating the family from the effects of the market. The marginalisation of the workforce, and of the households which comprise it, in a depressed region like the North East is emphasised by the higher levels of dependency on state benefits. Given the low level of wages in such a region, welfare intervention tends to mean that 'the part of the surplus population which is not of immediate interest as far as labour demand is concerned is maintained in a "frozen" state' (Mingione 1985:16), since the differential between benefit levels and wages in the case of those jobs which are available may be insufficient to provide a purely economic incentive to undertake employment. This, of course, is used as an argument by those on the New Right to reduce benefits. But the state is also involved in structuring low pay, and intervening in the market system here. It does this first through payment of family income supplement (now income support) to families on low incomes, second, through intervening to restrict trade union power whilst at the same time reducing restrictions on employers, and lastly through paying low wages to those on government employment schemes.

Many of the families in the Wearside sample were subject to the 'poverty trap' – or more specifically the 'unemployment trap' – thanks either to the low earnings disregard for families on supplementary benefit, or to men not being entitled to any benefit because of their wives' earnings. Setting the scene has shown how Mr Bradshaw reacts to the latter position. It is the combination of the unemployment trap with women's low pay which undermines the incentive for families to move towards role-reversal as a response to male unemployment, and encourages the polarisation of households into those where husbands and wives are both in employment, and households where neither is in employment. My Wearside sample was surprising in two respects. First, women did work despite the restrictions of the benefit system and their own low earnings. Second, the number of hours that some women were prepared to work was unexpectedly high. The popular conception of low paid female workers is that they are uncommitted to the labour market. This was certainly not the case for the majority of women in my sample: not merely were many prepared to work despite the disincentives of the benefit system and of low pay, but also of hours worked and length of time in current job indicated a substantial commitment to the labour market. In addition, as we have already seen, a number of women discussed their jobs in considerable detail, and with obvious enthusiasm, while a number of husbands also appreciated how much their wives loved their jobs (see also Stubbs and Wheelock 1989).

The financial reality for many of the sample wives and their families serves to underline their commitment to the labour market yet again. This can be analysed in terms of the five groups that husbands fall into with respect to type of benefit or other income received: those receiving unemployment benefit, supplementary benefit, no benefit at all, invalidity benefit, and the two husbands receiving a wage or a pension. Only in the last case was there no restriction on their wives' earnings, and correspondingly, in one of these families the wife worked full time. There were six families where the husband was on supplementary benefit, the most restrictive category for wives earning, since any income over £4 was deducted from the husband's benefit. Two of the wives in this group acted as 'rational economic women', since they worked very few hours, one having reduced her hours substantially in response to the earnings rule. However, three more wives worked around 18 to 20 hours, and one worked full-time. There is obviously a very substantial financial disincentive to work such long hours under these circumstances.

A further eight families had husbands on unemployment benefit, where the financial disincentive on women working was less. It is nevertheless worth pointing out that all these families happened to have dependent children, which means that the husband was entitled to a supplementary benefit top up if his wife was not earning. This was probably at least part of the reason why two of the wives in this group had given up work, again behaving in an economically rational fashion. For two other wives, it was clearly worth their families' while for them to work, one because she worked full-time, the other because she was one of the few women who was well paid. Since the two remaining wives neither worked long hours, nor earned very much, the financial gain from working was unlikely to be substantial, and may have been negative.

In the eleven families in which the husband was on invalidity benefit, there were few financial disincentives to wives working, given on the one hand that only one of these wives worked full-time and on the other that only one was well paid in hourly terms. This meant that only two wives had deductions for earning more that the £45 allowed under the invalidity benefit rules. For the final category, the advantages and disadvantages of wives working when this results in their husbands receiving no benefit are not easy to assess. In all three of these families, the wives were working full-time, but earning only low wages, so that the income differential between the wife working and the family relying on the benefit system could not have been great and might well have been negative, especially given that two of the families had dependent children. Probably as great an economic disincentive in the long run was that the husband in such families was at the time not entitled to employment on a government scheme.

The empirical evidence just examined suggests a third model for negotiations over the gender division of household work strategies in addition to the traditional and the economic rationality models: a model of self-respect. In a substantial proportion of the sample – some ten families in all – wives continued to work despite the fact that the family was at best only very marginally better off, and in some cases was actually worse off as a result. Whilst the present government is anxious to present a picture of scrounging and dependence on the state, legislation actually encourages the traditional patriarchal attitudes which undermine families' ability to act in an economically rational manner. Recent legislative changes have made little difference to this picture, though ironically, the new regulations no longer regard a cooker as a necessity for families, who loose their self-reliance still more by being forced into the market economy and queueing in their local fish and chip shop for their meals instead of cooking in their own home. Yet the concern for self-respect, in some of the sample families at least, was sufficiently strong to overcome both economic rationality and traditional attitudes.

The potential for conflict within families where husbands are not working and their wives are in low paid work is thus high. Not merely are households the arena within which the gender conflict between the economic rationality demands of capitalism and the traditional demands of a patriarchal rationality is playing itself out; the household is also the focus for resolving the conflict between market rationality and the urge towards self-reliance and independence from the state. In households where men have become unemployed, it is wives who hold the key to the self-respect which the family can obtain by irrationally working in the labour market in order to avoid dependence on the welfare system, itself in conflict with traditional views of the gender division of labour. Despite Wearside men taking on new roles which by no means correspond to traditional stereotypes, adjustment to non-employment is not easy since the potential for conflict within the family is large. Little wonder that such adjustment should be seen as a second-best path by both wives and husbands.

Household work strategies, then, and negotiations between the sexes over such strategies, are not merely adopted in response to market forces, but also to pressures from traditional views and from the state, these two reinforcing each other; as well as arising from the family's sense of self-respect. Market forces themselves are in any case not purely economic in nature, but are affected by the historical development of the gender division of labour, which can both be reinforced by traditional ideology and actually masked by it. In seeking self-respect, families are on the one hand keeping the market at bay through the development of inter-personal relations within the household which lead to a household work strategy which conflicts with economic rationality. On the other hand, they are keeping the state at bay by attempting to avoid dependence on the welfare state as far as possible, where again the household work strategy conflicts with economic rationality, as well as with the traditional rationality incorporated in the benefit system. This can be seen as the adoption of a personalised family life style as opposed to a public one. Yet it is a process of personal privatisation not merely with respect to the state, but also with respect to the market.

In wider terms, the self-respect model as a basis for negotiation over the gender pattern of household work strategies indicates that a material theory of human needs is inadequate. This is of course something that many people, including certain economists, have been aware of anyway. As Jane Humphries puts it: 'Thus the family, as an institution, has been shaped by the aspiration of people for personalized non-market methods of distribution and social interaction' (in Amsden 1980:154). Pahl and Wallace see this in terms of a domestic life style, where 'domestication' is 'the product of a value system which puts home-centred activities as the central focus of a distinctive life-style' (1985:219), with self-provisioning, and an enlarging of work within the domestic economy, flowing largely, but not entirely from a home-centred value orientation. Pahl and Wallace contrast the way in which self-respect links in with an enlarged domestic economy at the more affluent end of the working-class income scale with unemployed households. They see the former as a 'dependent domesticity' in the sense that it relies on the wages of multiple earners in a declining labour market.

My own research shows working-class households who are in an intermediate position, with certain of them being able to move towards a household work strategy allowing for self-respect for the family and for the individuals within it, through gender congruence in the complementary and the formal economies. On the one hand, this is a gender congruent version of Pahl and Wallace's household work strategy; on the other, it is also an 'independent domesticity'. Self-respect in this case is pursued regardless of market and state welfare pressures.

Conclusions: 'rational economic families'?

One of the classic assumptions of economics is that time and income are substitutes for each other. This assumption lies behind the long-cherished idea of economists that work is a 'disutility', and that people therefore need to be paid a wage or salary to persuade them to give up leisure time. There is, in other words, an opportunity cost to participating in the labour force in terms of leisure foregone. As was seen in Chapter 3, Gary Becker (1965) and the new home economics school provide a revised theory of consumer choice that treats all commodities symmetrically by stressing only their differences in relative time and earning intensities. This means that both market work and domestic work can be seen as contributing to the production of basic commodities yielding utility, while leisure is desirable in its own right. Households are then assumed to allocate time so as to maximise returns. If a household member works at home, this is because returns from unpaid housework are perceived as equal to or higher than those from market work for that individual.

Commentators have pointed out that this opportunity cost approach can be problematic because the real world does not necessarily give people the option of making choices about the use of marginal hours, or even total hours. Indeed, for neither the affluent nor the unemployed do time and income appear to be substitutes for each other. The 'harried leisure class', to use Linder's (1970) apt terminology, have substantial incomes, but a shortage of time. As Burns so pithily expresses it: 'For most of us, affluence is the privilege of waiting for help in a department store, searching for a parking spot' (Burns 1977:171). For the individuals who make up the success story of Thatcher's Britain, time is the final scarcity: for the fate of those with higher than average incomes, is to be trapped in isolated pockets of temporal scarcity. The dogmatic emphasis of the New Right on the importance of material incentives ignores the fact that larger incomes cannot buy time.

Chancellor Lawson's 1988 budget, in substantially reducing taxation for the rich strengthened their monetary incentives. This does not deal with temporal poverty, but gives the already materially better off the limited satisfaction of being able to purchase still more goods. The Yuppie lifestyle can be seen as a modification of the conspicuous consumption and waste posited by Thorstein Veblen at the turn of the century. He pointed out that the struggle for wealth is different from the struggle for subsistence, in that the former is concerned with emulation. Waste then becomes the common characteristic necessary for demonstrating the possession of wealth. The recent budget, then, encourages pecuniary emulation and thus conspicuous waste where 'articles are to an extent preferred for use on account of their being conspicuously wasteful; they are felt to be serviceable somewhat in proportion as they are wasteful and ill-adapted to their ostensible use' (Veblen 1912:126). Veblen argues that emulation is second only to self-preservation as the strongest of economic motives: small wonder then that in promoting a narrowly economic rationality for the already well off, the spending boom should continue and Britain's balance of payments move further into the red. There is an inevitably inflationary effect in boosting what has to be conspicuous consumption for a harried leisure class whose real shortage is time rather than income.

The underside of the success story of Thatcherite Britain is the underclass of unemployed families who have too much time and not enough income. Here again, material wealth and temporal wealth are mutually exclusive, but from the opposite starting point. For families where the man is unemployed, the state benefit system suppresses economic rationality and confirms patriarchal rationality and the gender bias of the market mechanism. The spatial impact of the changing economic structure means that marginal opportunities for unemployed men and women are often not available in terms of self-employment or the irregular economy any more than wage earning. The New Right focuses on the idea of self-help and the role of the individual in the market, yet in practice the unit is the family, and it is within families that decisions are made about work strategies. The institutional framework of state welfare and low pay, especially for women, tends to structure whole families into unemployment. Unemployed families with low incomes and ample time are the opposite side of the coin of those enjoying success in 1980s Britain. For neither the timeless unemployed nor the harried leisure class are time and income substitutes for one another.

But perhaps it is unfair to the opportunity cost model to take the two extremes of the income spectrum. Pahl and Wallace looked at another category of families who might be considered Thatcherite success stories: two-earner, working-class, owner-occupier families in the South. The surprise from this study is that paid and unpaid work appeared as complementary. Employment and work in the complementary economy went together, and 'There is an indication that people actually *choose* to do this domestic work' (Pahl and Wallace 1985:215). Such a choice is not understandable from the standpoint of pure economic rationality, even if it is accepted that perceptions of economic rationality may differ between men and women. It is a gender differentiated economic rationality which is *modified* by the adoption of a self-reliant home centred life style. Certain economic conditions – the availability of employment – are a necessary, but not a sufficient condition for adopting this domestic life style, which is thus undoubtedly moulded by economic circumstances, but not determined by them.

My own empirical work seems to indicate a group which exists despite Thatcher's New Right, in that some families are adopting a work strategy based on a self-respect which actually conflicts with economic rationality. As a result of economic restructuring in the regions there has been a change in the balance of gender power and authority within the household which has meant a shift in work strategies for men and women within households in a gender congruent direction. This movement has taken place not merely in opposition to economic rationality in some cases, but also despite pressures from traditional views of roles and from the state. The self-respect model of family motivation tends to be associated with a gender congruent life style which involves sharing between husband and wife. Work for such families is not seen as a disutility, but instead self-respect is being derived from paid and unpaid work. Wives – and to some extent husbands – are deriving self-respect from female participation in paid work whilst men are able to gain a rather lesser degree of self-respect from unpaid work. As employment opportunities have altered, men have become economically less powerful and their wives more so, thus changing the balance of the domestic bargain in favour of women. Feminists, whether women or men, may see hope for a less gender segregated future arising from the changing behaviour of this group.

However, as the last section has shown, the presence of conflicting rationalities tends to focus economic and social conflict within the family, though my empirical work was not designed to identify the possible long-term effects of this on families. Effectively the market mechanism and the economic individualism of the New Right are structured so that any individuals or families who base their decision-making on self-respect will at best be taken for granted, at worst taken advantage of or exploited by the economic system within which they find themselves. Goldschmidt-Clermont (1987) draws attention to the fact that the concept of maximising returns is culturally bound, so that the concept of opportunity cost is of limited use in Third World societies where conformity to tradition and community life and support are valued, as opposed to societies where the value of achievement, competition, personal initiative, and social mobility are praised. But my own research, and that of Pahl and Wallace (1985) for instance, indicate that there may be varying value systems within families in developed capitalist economic formations too, reflected in the adoption of different life styles. The value of self-respect cannot readily be assessed in terms of the value of saving time. Yet families are left to pick up the pieces for themselves when internal conflict is the result of a value system of self-respect; such conflict is in terms of economic jargon, an externality for a Thatcherite market.

In order to reduce conflict within the family and to harness people's sense of self-respect, economic rationality and self-respect need to be brought into line with each other in a humanised incentive system, which does not simple rely on selfish monetary rewards. This could be done by a concerted and effective effort to make institutional changes to reduce the conflict introduced by low pay, by the state benefit system, by the taxation system, and by owner-occupation. There would also need to be a genuine attempt to reduce the impact of patriarchal rationality. Proper recognition for the motive of self-respect can only be achieved by considering the family as a whole, and in particular both sexes within it, rather than the individual. There is thus finally a need to bring economic rationality into line between men and women. As things stand at the present moment, the family has relatively little choice in terms of its work strategy; it is inflexible due to the framework within which it is placed, where economic and patriarchal constraints render it unadaptable. Labour market rigidities not only prevent labour-substitution within the market, but also substitution of market for non-market work for low paid, working-class women. Rigidities in performing domestic activities also mean that paid work and unpaid work are complementary in many ways. This means that for many families there is not even choice with regard to all hours, let alone marginal hours. Such lack of choice makes for a sense of helplessness and alienation. I have looked at a minority of families who *have* adapted their work strategies in non-traditional and economically irrational ways. Society will be the better if motivations based on self-respect and gender congruence can be encouraged by giving them economic rewards, rather than being economically discouraged. Families need to be allowed to forge their own life-style of self-reliance, without it being at variance with economic rationality.

In broader terms, such a system would be one which reduces the mutual exclusiveness of time and wealth. It would be less alienating because it would allow of proper consideration of a *total* work strategy which takes account of *all* forms of work, and not simply of reasonably paid male work. Whilst the orthodox economic paradigm views work as a disutility within a framework that considers only purely economic motivations, a Marxist paradigm integrates work activity into the development of the whole human being. For whilst it is true that the majority of Marx's economic analysis is concerned with capitalist development as a process of creating material wealth, he is also concerned to ask how material wealth becomes *real* wealth through the all-sided and full development of each individual. Julkunen (1977) has shown that Marx ultimately reduced the whole of economics to the economy of time, and a development of his analysis makes it possible to link the allocation of time with the development of personality.

The historical evolution of capitalism was examined by Marx as the saving of living labour, so that the saving of labour time is identical with the development of the productive forces. Making a comparison between developed and underdeveloped countries, Julkunen suggests that the capitalist economy was the first economy of conscious time-saving, and that from the basic law of value and capitalist competition springs the urge to minimize the consumption of working time. It is this which allows of the growth of material wealth, but the saving of living labour also forms the basis for the emergence of disposable time, which can be used for the creation of new material and spiritual needs. However,

> in the economy of working time, off-work time has only a peripheral status. The principle of time saving of off-work time is important only insofar as it ensures the sufficient reproduction of human vital power as regards the work process.
>
> (Julkunen 1977:11)

The full development of each individual is only possible when work no longer appears as work, but as the full development of human activity itself. This personality development is only possible if both the society as a whole and the individuals within it allocate time in the right proportions to all activities, not simply in terms of paid working time, but of the entire time fund of the society and the individual. At this stage, it is not sufficient to think in terms of purely individual economic motivations, and wider aspirations for fulfilling other aspects of what it is to be a human being must be brought into play. 'In the spirit of Marxist tradition socialist research on leisure time and official ideology have emphasised that leisure time is time which ensures harmonious personality development' (Julkunen 1977:13).

On the basis of Marx's analysis, Julkunen suggests that the process of economic development involves the development of a sense of time. The paradox is that with more highly developed productive resources, time becomes relatively more expensive and valuable, so that the more time is saved the scarcer it becomes. It is for this reason that poverty and scarcity do not appear as a lack of time in underdeveloped conditions. One of the major cultural conflicts between European colonisers and those whom they colonised arose from different perceptions of time. The colonisers had a strongly developed sense of time deriving from the importance for capitalism of saving scarce time, but for the poor in the colonies, time was not scarce. Within developed economies themselves a similar dichotomy can be observed, where the unemployed have no scarcity of time. The social experiences of the employed and the unemployed are thus very different because there is no external necessity for the latter to maintain their sense of time. There is a similar gulf between the employed and the unemployed as there is between the rulers of empire and the ruled. However in the case of the unemployed, they are distinguished from the rest of society by the poverty of their temporal experience. What they do with their time is not of significance to society as a whole, provided they do not resort to criminal activities. It is in this sense that the unemployed are an 'underclass'. Indeed when Jahoda (1982) says that, as well as its financial rewards, a job has certain latent functions in providing access to important categories of experience, she is essentially arguing that employment renders time valuable, and therefore scarce.

The problems that the unemployed face in adapting, express themselves primarily in terms of 'too much time', for time has ceased to be scarce for them. But the theory of personality sketched out by the French Marxist Lucien Séve based on Marx's theses of personality and the economy of time suggests that we can go further in exploring the effect of unemployment on personality. Séve argues that 'personality appears as the "accumulation" of the most varied activities in time' (Julkunen

1977:13). The infrastructure of personality is formed on the basis of individual activity, which must be a temporal structure. Séve sees two dimensions to activity, the first involving the contrast between sector I activity where learning activities are undertaken and sector II in which learning is used to gratify needs. (This parallels Marx's distinction between economic departments I and II where means of production and articles of consumption are respectively located.) The other dimension distinguishes abstract and concrete work; abstract activity is alienated activity, subject to external necessity, while concrete activity is un-alienated, personal activity.

For those in employment, abstract, alienated needs gratification activity looms largest in the individual's time plan. For the unemployed, concrete, unalienated, personal activity will become at least proportionately more significant. Problems in adaptation arise because such activity is often trivial, and because it is through abstract activity that individuals come into contact with developed productive forces and culture. For the employed, on the other hand, conflict arises from over-emphasis on activities which are subject to selfish monetary motivations. It is interesting that in the wake of what many have seen as an obscene budget handout to the rich, the Thatcher government seems to have been groping towards a realisation that a reliance on selfish monetary motivations is not sufficient, and the better off have been urged to donate some of their budget benefits to good causes. The market mechanism demands the pursuit of self-interest. But nineteenth century-style charity from large companies and rich citizens cannot prevent the pursuit of self-interest from undermining the self-respect of employed and unemployed alike. Only a radical rethink can bring individual morality and the market mechanism into line with each other, by taking account of a non-material theory of human needs.

Conclusions

Monopoly capitalism, the domestic economy, and the changing nature of work

The last chapter has already drawn out many of the implications of my empirical work for economic theory. To conclude this study, I should therefore like to sketch out a framework within which the effects of national and international changes in the nature of monopoly capitalism on household work strategies can be considered. How, in other words, is an economic system within which the domestic and voluntary sectors are to be incorporated, regulated? Throughout this book, I have been concerned to demonstrate the wide range of interrelationships that exist between the social and the formal economies. Many of them involve important gender dimensions. Yet, despite the substantial weight of the domestic sector within the economy as a whole, it has rarely been adequately incorporated within economic models.

This, I would suggest, is because the domestic sector cannot be readily understood within an orthodox theoretical paradigm. In addition, despite the attention that has been paid to gender issues in recent years, this has not been sufficiently incorporated into important aspects of the interrelationship between the social and formal economies. Much of this inadequacy can be understood in terms of the way that economics has been concerned to maintain its position as 'queen' (*sic*) of the social sciences by taking an aggressively separatist stance in relation to other disciplines. To be able to incorporate gender into the discipline would require economists to acknowledge the importance of taking an interdisciplinary approach to their subject matter, something that only Marxists and Institutionalists are prepared to do.

Chapter 1 developed a typology of productive economic institutions, highlighting the significance of the domestic sector within total economic activity and arguing the complementary nature of the relationship between the two. To understand how the economic system is regulated, I should like to return to this framework and elaborate it rather further. This will help to highlight the interrelations between the social and formal economies. Figure C.1, a variant of Figure 1.1 from the first chapter, shows some of the similarities and differences between the

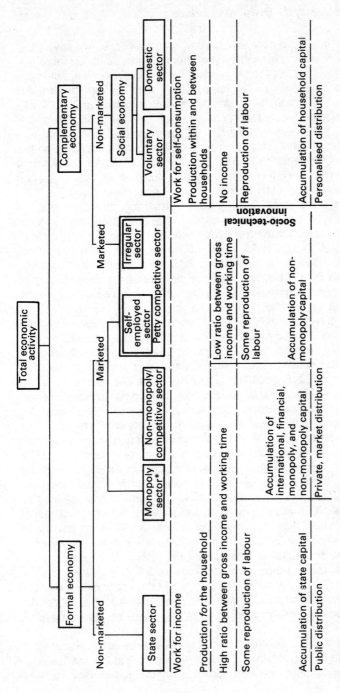

Figure C.1 Selected characteristics of economic sectors

* Includes international and financial capital

sectors of these two economies. First, whilst work, as we have seen, takes place throughout the whole economy, it can be divided into two types. In the social economy, work is for self-consumption, but in the rest of the economy – the formal economy, together with the irregular sector – work is undertaken for the income which is earned. Whilst production in the latter case is production *for* the household, in the social economy, production is also taking place: in this case within and between households. The domestic sector involves production within households; the voluntary sector, between them. Whilst many might regard the market as the core of the production process, a consideration of total economic activity thus shows it to be an intermediary.

Second, this interrelationship has a further significance in that the combination of work for self-consumption and work for income 'constitutes the reason for the connection between the reproductive cycle of the unit and the general process of accumulation or development' (Mingione 1985:25). Now in Chapter 2, structural economic change was analysed in the light of the changing patterns of the accumulation of capital and of the reproduction of labour and capital within the capitalist world economy. Figure C.1 summarises the role that the different sectors of the economy play in these respects. The social economy plays a primary role in the production and reproduction of labour, with its responsibility for the care of children, the elderly, the sick, and the disabled. The domestic sector also accumulates substantial amounts of household capital (Burns 1977; Gershuny 1978). The state sector of the formal economy plays a far smaller role in the reproduction of labour through its health and education services, and accumulates capital in the form of state capital. Monopoly and non-monopoly sectors together play a very important role in the accumulation of capital, whether it takes the form of international, financial, monopoly, or non-monopoly capital.

In terms of reproduction, it makes sense to consider the irregular sector as part of a petty competitive sector which includes the self-employed sector of the formal economy. This sector is characterised by the very small scale of its units whose status as a form of capital is ambivalent. Both the irregular and the self-employed sectors provide an outlet for what Marx termed the industrial reserve army, who may or may not be successful in establishing themselves as capitalist entrepreneurs in the non-monopoly sector, so avoiding a return to unemployment or employment. What distinguishes this sector from the rest of the marketed sectors is that it incorporates not only the possibility of the accumulation of non-monopoly capital, but also the reproduction of labour.

Chapter 2 pointed out that changing patterns of accumulation on a world scale affect patterns of employment, Indeed, in the last few decades the capitalist world has become a single labour market (Godfrey

1986:23). The chapter highlighted gender changes in the overall volume of employment, in its distribution between sectors and industries, and in its occupational distribution, together with their spatial implications. Global restructuring of capital has also meant radical changes in the division of labour through a restructuring of the labour process. In a modern industrialised society, labour is divided in a number of different ways, which all interact with each other (Purcell *et al.* 1986:3). First there is the fragmentation and co-ordination of tasks within a particular work situation, which, second, contrasts with the differentiation and co-operation between particular jobs and professions in a given society. Thirdly there is an international division of labour between the employment structures of the First and Third Worlds, and finally there is the division between domestic and paid work. Thus, not only did Chapter 2 show changes in the structure of employment, but also radical alterations in the divisions of labour within Britain in the post-war period. It explored the social, gender, and spatial restructuring that has taken place as the organisation of the labour process altered with changing patterns of accumulation.

One outcome of the analysis in Chapter 2 was to suggest that employment structure is becoming more characterised by fragmentation, particularly along gender lines, but including rises in self-employment, unemployment, and flexible working for both men and women. This can be represented in terms of differences in the costs of reproduction between different sectors of the economy. Labour in the social economy is not paid, since it involves work for self-consumption. In the state, monopoly and non-monopoly sectors there tends to be a high ratio between gross income and working time, whilst in the petty competitive sector there is a low ratio between gross income and working time (Mingione 1985:30). Labour market fragmentation is part of the process of competition between different forms of capital, including international capital. Competition also involves differences in the costs of reproduction within sectors, as well as between them.

The household, as the unit of reproduction, must apply its working activities to earning and to directly supplying goods and services through self-consumption. Household work strategies require the individuals who make up this unit to negotiate and decide a balance between work for income and for self-consumption. These decisions will however be made in the light of the social and gender recompositions brought about by the process of international economic restructuring. Such restructuring involves an articulated combination of the reproduction of labour power and of capital. The result will be to rearticulate the gender divisions of labour within the household. Pressures to change the division of labour are likely to be particularly great in regions where male unemployment in high and where opportunities for female employment are relatively buoyant, and Chapter 4 described such a process of change in the Wearside local economy.

Any rearticulation of work strategies within the household is subject to four major constraints: economic rationality, pressures from the state benefit system, traditional ideology, and the desire for self-respect. Women and men, as we saw in Chapter 3, have different perceptions of economic rationality. On the one hand, economic rationality must take account of employment opportunities, levels of pay and access to state benefits for both husband and wife. On the other, economic rationality will also be coloured by the unequal access that women and men have to the family wage. At the same time, the Keynes-Beveridge framework for state intervention in the labour market has proven particularly poorly adapted for the changing structure of employment since the Second World War. It was based on an assumption that a husband could earn an adequate wage to support his family. The secular change in the identity of the typical wage earner has undermined that possibility. The state has thus done much to buttress concepts of a continuing traditional gender division of labour within the household. Yet economic restructuring has undermined the economic basis of such traditional ideology in a number of important, if somewhat ambivalent, ways. Finally, Chapter 5 has shown that families may decide household work strategies on the basis of self-respect, involving a desire to be free both from the constraints of the market and from the state benefit system; a self-respect which may also fly in the face of traditional rationalities. Under these circumstances, wives may decide to work in the formal economy, whilst their husbands become more involved in the social economy, the result of which is a more gender congruent division of labour.

A household work strategy based on self-respect can be understood in terms of a reconceptualisation of the labour process. The labour process within the household involves the adoption of a personalised life style. Indeed, one of the hall marks of the social economy is that it allows of the development of a personalised life style, based on home centred values, which, as we saw in the last chapter, may be at variance with economic rationality. In contrast, the marketed sectors of the economy satisfy private, rather than personal needs, needs which are directly circumscribed by market based values.

Indeed, different sectors of the economy satisfy different needs: the state provides for collective needs, the market for private needs and the social economy for personal needs, corresponding to different systems of distribution. A distribution system depends upon differing levels of commodification between sectors: in the social economy there is a personalised system of distribution, which can be contrasted with the private, market based system of the monopoly, non-monopoly, and petty competitive sectors, and the public distribution of the state sector. The boundaries between the institutional mechanisms by which the three types of needs – collective, private, and personal – are met are of course porous and variable. For example, the collective need for education or health can also be supplied through the market, as is made very clear by the New Right, or indeed within the domestic or the voluntary sectors. Personal needs can and are transformed into private needs through the medium of advertising by the market sectors.

By talking in terms of personal needs and the development of a personalised life style, I am not denying the importance of household work strategies as survival mechanisms. Indeed, the balance between work for self-consumption and for income is a function of the qualitative and quantitative structure of labour demand. But the relation between the family and occupational structure goes beyond survival strategy to the importance of the division of labour in the domestic unit. The domestic unit 'filters the demand and regulates the supply of labour in the market' (Connolly 1985:80). The domestic unit may choose to adopt a personal life style in addition. It is worth noting also that the petty competitive sector is unique in that a combination of private and personal needs can be met here. Whilst many might regard this sector as exploited by those forms of capital which have accumulated into larger units, individuals may choose to work in this sector, not merely as a survival strategy, but because they prefer the life style that this work incorporates, perhaps particularly in terms of 'being their own boss'.

Institutionalists argue that value theory is a study of the process by which judgements about values are made. It is important to realise that such judgements are made in the context of the dynamic process of technological accumulation.

> The innovation and use of the better and more desirable technologies is a process that occasions changes in the structure of institutions and in their behaviour norms, which those institutions are imposing on individuals. And those institutionalized behaviour norms are the values of institutions and in turn are affecting the values of individuals.
>
> (Adams 1980:37)

There is thus a process of self-correcting value judgements, against a background of technological change. The household is significant as an institution within which such judgements are made, and Gershuny (1978, 1983) puts forward a theory of socio-technical innovation which provides a framework for linking the domestic sector to the formal economy.

Gershuny points out that the connection between needs and economic demand is not a direct one, but rather mediated by technology. A socio-technical innovation is one where the means by which a need is satisfied changes, so that households' demand for commodities change too. There are new modes of provision for particular needs; and instead of catching the bus to work, people buy cars which they drive themselves. Socio-technical innovations like the private motor car, television, video-recorders, washing machines, freezers, and microwaves, have a two-fold effect. First the new modes of provision for particular needs affect the structure of the economy through final demand, while secondly they influence the division between paid and unpaid time and thus household activity patterns. Gershuny's theory suggests not merely an interrelation between the household sector and the formal economy, but that the domestic sector may well be a causal factor for economic development. Such a shift to the domestic provision of services also has important gender implications, of which Gershuny is aware, although he does not develop them. They have been brought out in this book.

There are thus three important implications for economic theory arising from the arguments put forward in this book. First, economic maximisation is not sufficient as a rationale for economic activity. Some professional economists, not to mention many students when they are first introduced to economic concepts, have an intuitive antipathy to *homo economicus*, and not simply on the basis of the sexism that is implied, though that in itself is significant enough. Veblen (1912) labelled orthodox economic man as 'that spinning globule of desire', while Gruchy 'found the orthodox conception of man repugnant: amoral, hedonistic, deficient in not admitting of mutual empathy, unappreciative of individual and cultural differences . . . knowing all but understanding nothing' (in Adams 1980:12). For Hollis and Nell, rational economic man is rarely portrayed, but introduced furtively:

> We do not know what he wants. But we do know that whatever it is, he will maximise ruthlessly to get it . . . as consumer he maximizes utility by omniscient and improbable comparison of, for instance, marginal strawberries with marginal cement.
>
> (Hollis and Nell 1975:54)

My study of Wearside families indicates that such moral and philosophical arguments against 'rational economic man' are supported by empirical evidence. The individual units of economic analysis, households – more widely known as families – may make their decisions about work strategies on the basis of self-respect, and not simply on the basis of economic rationality, whether or not this is modified by traditional views of the division of labour.

The second important implication is that households, or families, should not be considered as a single unit as they are in economics, but rather appreciated as a group who bear the brunt of the contradictions arising from the need to reconcile the conflicting rationalities of self-respect, traditional views, and the rationality imposed by the market. Economic and social conflict thus become focused on the family. Not merely does the market avoid the costs of such conflict, the market actually gains in terms of people's desire to work even though it may be economically irrational to do so. Structural change in the economy is in any case mediated within the family through differentiated gender perceptions of economic rationality. The last chapter suggested some broad policy measures which would encourage motivations based on self-respect and gender congruence by giving such motivations economic rewards, and encouraging families to develop their own life style of self-reliance without it being at variance with economic rationality.

The final implication is that it is not possible to separate either the domestic sector or the social economy from the formal economy. The social economy is neither at the margins of reproduction nor of accumulation, and indeed the complementary and the formal economies combine in provisioning society. The boundary between the formal and the social economy is established by how production decisions within the household are made, but households use multiple work strategies, so that this also provides the link between the complementary and the formal economy. However, the decisions that households make are not necessarily on the basis of economic maximisation. So whilst the regulatory system within the social economy cannot be independent of that within the formal international capitalist system, it does have a separate pole. True, work for self-consumption within the social economy may be a coping response to inadequate resources and entirely a function of economic constraints. But there may also be work for self-consumption which allows a personalised life style and a sense of creativeness.

In terms of regulation of the total economic system, there is thus an enigmatic interaction between the social and the formal economy. This is because on the one hand work within the social economy may be the result of the market constraints of increasing poverty; on the other hand it may be the result of increasing affluence and a relative separation from economic constraints represented by the adoption of a personalised life style. The interaction is rendered all the more ambivalent by the fact that even some of the least well off – and the Wearside families certainly fell into this category – may choose to base their work strategies and their life style on self-respect. The intimate relationship between the formal and the complementary economies means that the mode of regulation of monopoly capitalism is modified by the personal wishes and aspirations put into effect within the social economy. The labour process debate emphasised the importance of work as a relation between human beings as well as an economic category. A study of the labour process within the household indicates that women and men may partially liberate themselves from market forces by choosing a gender-congruent work strategy which incorporates a personalised life style at variance with economic and traditional rationalities alike.

The effect of international changes in the nature of monopoly capitalism on household work strategies are mediated through gender perceptions of economic rationality, and based on intra-household negotiations over the division of labour, which will also be coloured by traditional, patriarchal views. The regional concentration of economic decline and restructuring mean that in developed economies the issue of changing gender roles appears in a particularly stark form in declining regions. There are indeed constraints on challenges to gender identity, but there is evidence of work as a meaningful and purposive activity for both women and men which does something to overcome state and institutional constraints on role change, whilst economic constraints can do much to neutralise the force of traditional attitudes on the part of both sexes. It should be possible to develop policies that would encourage such shifts towards more gender congruent life styles.

My work has shown traditional gender roles breaking down in North East working-class families, when men become unemployed, but their wives remain at work. What might this mean in terms of trends for the future, and what are the implications for policy? There has been a strong regional bias in the recent process of economic recovery. This study has shown families in the North East who are constrained by a harsh economic reality, and whilst they are in a minority, the pressures seem likely to continue. Commentators are uncertain as to the long run viability of British recovery, a recovery which has in any case had a far less marked effect on the regions. On Wearside, the closure of the shipyards will push male unemployment rates up again. Nationally, the constraints on claiming benefit are becoming more severe. Yet at the same time, the downward pressure on the lowest wages, inevitably those of women in particular, continues with especial force in the regions. The incentive system at the lowest end of the income scale has rather become one of increasing disincentives, in reality a punishment system which operates with particular force in the regions.

Does this mean that a feminist or progressive strategy should be campaigning for male unemployment and supporting harsher benefit criteria? I have already argued at the end of the last chapter that this is not the way forward. True, my results show a marked shift in the direction of gender congruence if wives of unemployed men can be persuaded to continue to go out to work. However, such effects also have a strong negative impact: they increase conflict within the family by relying on the family's sense of self-respect being stronger than their response to economic rationality. The situation is only made the more problematic by the institutional constraints which mean that the economically rational is not the same for women as it is for men.

It would not be easy to propose a specific set of legislative changes to encourage the gender congruent changes in roles which have been brought about by the harsh economic realities of the Wearside economy. It is however possible to suggest a set of criteria to govern policy proposals. First, it is important to reduce the impact of patriarchal rationality by bringing economic rationality into line between women and men, and encouraging motivations based on gender congruence. This would involve institutional changes to reduce the conflict introduced by low pay, the state benefit system and the taxation system.

Second, people's sense of self-respect needs to be harnessed through a humanised incentive system which brings economic rationality and self-respect into line with each other, and does not simply rely on selfish monetary rewards. The New Right's 'active citizen' is a crude attempt to graft public spiritedness on to a new patriarchy involving a return to family values in the private domain and to the enterprise economy in the public one. Yet the self-reliance that is the keynote in the two domains, can only be purged of its selfish nature by being linked with the closely-related concept of mutual aid. It is essential to develop institutions in both the public and the private sectors of the economy which integrate the concepts of self-help with those of mutual aid, with participation in decision making as the key.

Finally, such policy principles will only be effective if they are placed in a context within which there is a concern to reduce the mutual exclusiveness of time and wealth. Proper consideration needs to be given to a total work strategy which takes account of all forms of work, not just reasonably paid male work, recognising that choices of life style are part and parcel of changes in the organisation of work. Within such a concern for making choices in overall work strategy for individual families possible, there must be more equitable sharing of decently paid employment on a geographical and a gender basis. Gender neutral policies for a shorter working week could make a significant contribution here, and explicit regional policies to shift the economic centre of gravity away from the South East would be essential.

Notes

Setting the scene 1

1 Further details can be found in Wheelock (1986).
2 The changing roles perspective is dealt with in more detail in Chapter 4, in the section headed Men's domestic roles.
3 The Employment Potential in Sunderland survey was undertaken in mid-1985, details of the survey are available in Howard *et al.* (1986).
4 My research collaborator, Kath Price and I did the interviews. We did the pilot interviews together.
5 The interview structure and the form of household and childcare tasks are reproduced in Wheelock (1986), or copies are available from the author on request.
6 The names of all the sample families have been changed to preserve anonymity.
7 Under the old benefit system then in force, if spouses earned over £4 per week, claimants had a pound for pound deduction from their supplementary benefit (DHSS leaflet SB.8/Nov. 1984).
8 Janet Finch comments on how easy it is for women researchers to elicit material from other women. I had the same experience with couples. I agree with her that there is a real exploitative potential in the relationship established between interviewer and interviewee. (See Finch in Bell and Roberts (eds) 1984:80.)
9 The Low Pay Unit defines low wages as at or below two-thirds of the median earning of a full-time male worker. This is close to the TUC minimum wage target, and to the Council of Europe's 'decency threshold.'
10 The Pilgrim Trust report of 1938 on *Men Without Work* does at times touch on the issue of household organisation, and one of the areas surveyed was the mining village of Crook in County Durham. The report's concerns in this respect however focus on how far wives of unemployed men are able to fulfil their traditional roles. 'It is equally plain that the good housekeeper has an enormous advantage over the bad, and that the answer to whether a family actually lives in poverty or not depends largely on the competence of the housewife' (Pilgrim Trust 1938:114). There is thus considerable discussion of the practice of

housekeeping, and of policies which might provide support for women, but no questioning of gender roles.

Chapter 4

1 It was Kath Price, my research collaborator, who developed this idea of a quantitative benchmark.
2 It may be remembered that one of the thirty interviews was a lengthy door-step interview, and in this case no form of household tasks was available.

Bibliography

Adams, J. (1980) *Institutionalist Economics*, The Hague: Nijhoff.
Aglietta, M. (1979) *A Theory of Capitalist Regulation*, London: New Left Books.
——(1982) 'World capitalism in the eighties', *New Left Review* 137.
Allen, S., Purcell, K., Waton, A., and Wood, S. (eds) (1986) *The Experience of Unemployment*, London: Macmillan.
Amsden, A. H. (ed.) (1980) *The Economics of Women and Work*, Harmondsworth: Penguin.
Armstrong, P., Glyn, A., and Harrison, J. (1984) *Capitalism Since World War II*, London: Fontana.
Ashton, D. N. (1986) *Unemployment Under Capitalism*, Brighton: Wheatsheaf.
Barrère-Maurisson, M. A. (1982) 'Education and women's occupational cycle', in K. Hvidtfelt, K. Jorgensen, and R. Neilsen (eds) *Strategies for Integrating Women into the Labour Market*, Copenhagen: Women's Research Centre in Social Sciences.
Barrett, M. and McIntosh, M. (1980) 'The "family wage": some problems for socialists and feminists', *Capital and Class* (Summer) 1.
Becker, G. (1965) 'A theory of the allocation of time', reprinted in A. M. Amsden (ed.) *The Economics of Women and Work*, Harmondsworth: Penguin.
Beechy, V. (1977) 'Some notes on female wage labour in capitalist production', *Capital and Class*, (Autumn) 3.
Bell, D. (1974) *The Coming of a Post-Industrial Society*, London: Heinemann.
Bell, C. and Roberts, H. (eds) (1984) *Social Researching: Politics, Problems, Practice*, London: Routledge & Kegan Paul.
Bertaux, D. (ed.) (1981) *Biography and Society*, London: Sage.
Beynon, H. and Blackburn, R. M. (1972) *Perceptions of Work*, Cambridge: Cambridge University Press.
Bradley, H. (1986) 'Work, home and the restructuring of jobs', in K. Purcell, S. Wood, A. Waton, and S. Allen (eds) *The Changing Experience of Employment*, London: Macmillan.
Bulmer, M. (1986) *Neighbours: the Work of Philip Abrams*, Cambridge: Cambridge University Press.
Burns, S. (1977) *The Household Economy*, Boston: Beacon Press.

Chaney, J. (1980) 'Social Networks and Job Information' report to Joint SSRC/EOC Research Committee.

Clarke, J., Critcher, C., and Johnson, R. (eds) (1979) *Working Class Culture*, London: Hutchinson.

Clinard, M. B. and Yeager, P. C. (1980) *Corporate Crime*, New York: Macmillan.

Close, P. and Collins, R. (eds) (1985) *Family and Economy in Modern Society*, London: Macmillan.

Cockburn, C. (1983) *Brothers: Male Dominance and Technological Change*, London: Pluto Press.

Connolly, P. (1985) 'The politics of the informal sector: a critique in N. Redclift and E. Mingione (eds) *Beyond Employment: Gender, Household and Subsistence*, Oxford: Blackwell.

Conran, S. (1975) *Superwoman*, London: Sidgwick & Jackson.

Cornuel, D. and Duriez, B. (1985) 'Local exchange and state intervention', in N. Redclift and E. Mingione (eds) *Beyond Employment: Gender, Household and Subsistence*, Oxford: Blackwell.

Coulson, M., Magas, B., and Wainwright, H. (1975) 'The housewife and her labour under capitalism', *New Left Review* 89.

Cragg, A. and Dawson, T. (1984) *Unemployed Women: A Study of Attitudes and Experience*, Dept. of Employment Research Paper no. 47.

Cumes, J. W. C. (1984) *The Reconstruction of the World Economy*, Melbourne: Longman Cheshire.

Cutler, T., Williams, K., and Williams, J. (1986) *Keynes, Beveridge and Beyond*, London: Routledge & Kegan Paul.

Delphy, C. (1984) *Close to Home*, London: Hutchinson.

Dex, S. (1987) *Women's Occupational Mobility*, London: Macmillan.

Dunford, M., Gedes, M., and Perrons, D. (1981) 'Regional policy and the crisis in the UK: a long-run perspective', *International Journal of Urban and Regional Research*, 5 (3).

Dunford, M. and Perrons, D. (1983) *The Arena of Capital*, London: Macmillan.

——(1986) 'The restructuring of the post-war British space economy', in R. Martin and B. Rowthorn (eds) *The Geography of De-industrialisation*, London: Macmillan.

Economist, The (1987) 'The shadow economy', 19 September.

Ekins, P. (ed.) (1986) *The Living Economy*, London: Routledge & Kegan Paul.

Evans, F. (1984) 'Women's unemployment: a domestic occupation?' unpublished Ph.D. thesis, University of Kent.

Ferman, L. A. and Berndt, L. E. (1981) 'The irregular economy', in S. Henry (ed.) *Can I have it in Cash?*, London: Astragal.

Finch, J. (1984) 'It's great to have someone to talk to: the ethics and politics of interviewing women', in C. Bell and H. Roberts (eds) *Social Researching: Politics, Problems, Practice*, London: Routledge & Kegan Paul.

Fothergill, S. and Gudgin, G. (1982) *Unequal Growth: Urban and Regional Employment Change in the UK*, London: Heinemann.

Bibliography

Freeman, C., Clarke, J., and Soete, L. (1982) *Unemployment and Technical Innovation*, London: Francis Pinter.

Galbraith, J. K. (1975) *Economics and the Public Purpose*, London: André Deutsch.

Gardiner, J. (1975) 'Women's domestic labour', *New Left Review* 89.

Gershuny, J. (1978) *After Industrial Society*, London: Macmillan.

——(1983) *Social Innovation and the Division of Labour*, Oxford: Oxford University Press.

Glyn, A. and Sutcliffe, B. (1972) *British Capitalism, Workers and the Profit Squeeze*, Harmondsworth: Penguin.

Godfrey, M. (1986) *Global Unemployment: the New Challenge to Economic Theory*, Brighton: Wheatsheaf.

Goldschmidt-Clermont, L. (1987) *Economic Evaluations of Unpaid Household Work*, Geneva: International Labour Organization.

Hakim, C. (1982) 'The social consequences of high unemployment', *Journal of Social Policy* 11 (4).

Hartmann, H. (1979) 'The unhappy marriage of Marxism and Feminism', *Capital and Class* 8.

Hatch, S. (1981) 'Informal caring institutions', in S. Henry (ed.) *Can I have it in Cash?*, London: Astragal.

Henry, S. (ed.) (1981) *Can I have it in Cash?* London: Astragal.

Henwood, F. and Wyatt, S. (1986) 'Women's work, technological change and shifts in the employment structure', in R. Martin and B. Rowthorn (eds) *The Geography of De-industrialisation*, London: Macmillan.

Himmelweit, S. and Mohun, S. (1977) 'Domestic labour and capital', *Cambridge Journal of Economics* 1 (1).

HMSO (1985) *General Household Survey*, London.

Hollis, M. and Nell, E. (1975) *Rational Economic Man*, Cambridge: Cambridge University Press.

Howard, J., Morris, M., Stevens, J., and Stone, I. (1986) *Employment and Unemployment on Wearside: A Report based on the 1985 Sunderland Household Survey*, Sunderland Polytechnic EDU for EEC/Borough of Sunderland.

Hudson, R. (1986) 'Producing an industrial wasteland: capital, labour and the State in North East England', in R. Martin and B. Rowthorn (eds) *The Geography of De-industrialisation*, London: Macmillan.

Hunt, P. (1978) 'Cash transactions and household tasks', *Sociological Review*, 26: 555–71.

Hvidtfelt, K., Jorgensen, K., and Neilsen, R. (eds) (1982) *Strategies for Integrating Women into the Labour Market*, Copenhagen: Women's Research Centre in Social Sciences.

Jahoda, M. (1982) *Employment and Unemployment: A Social–Psychological Analysis*, Cambridge: Cambridge University Press.

Julkunen, R. (1977) 'A contribution to the categories of social time and the economy of time', *Acta Sociologica* 20 (1).

Land, H. (1978) 'Who cares for the family?' *Journal of Social Policy*, 7 (3).

Lenin, V. I. (1916) *Imperialism, the Highest Stage of Capitalism* reprinted in *Selected Works* (1970), vol.1, Moscow: Progress Publishers.

170

Lewis, J. (1983) 'Women, work and regional development', *Northern Economic Review*, (Summer) 7.

Linder, S. B. (1970) *The Harried Leisure Class*, New York: Columbia University Press.

McKee, L. and Bell, C. (1984) 'His unemployment/her problem', paper presented at the British Sociological Association Conference.

McKee, L. and Bell, C. (1985) 'Marital and family relations in times of male unemployment', in B. Roberts, R. Finnegan, and D. Gallie (eds) *New Approaches to Economic Life*, Manchester: Manchester University Press.

Mandel, E. (1975) *Late Capitalism*, London: New Left Books.

Marshall, M. (1987) *Long Waves of Regional Development*, London: Macmillan.

Martin, J. and Roberts, C. (1984) *Women and Employment: A Lifetime Perspective*, London: HMSO.

Martin, R. and Rowthorn, B. (eds) (1986) *The Geography of De-industrialisation*, London: Macmillan.

Massey, D. (1979) 'In what sense a regional problem?' *Regional Studies* 13 (2).

——(1986) 'The legacy lingers on: the impact of Britain's international role on its internal geography', in R. Martin and B. Rowthorn (eds) *The Geography of De-industrialisation*, London: Macmillan.

Massey, D. and Meegan, R. (1982) *The Anatomy of Job Loss*, London: Methuen.

Meager, N. (1986) 'Temporary work in Britain', *Employment Gazette* (Jan.).

Miles, I. (1983) *Adaptation to Unemployment?*, University of Sussex, SPRU Occasional Paper 20.

Mingione, E. (1985) 'Social reproduction of the surplus labour force', in N. Redclift and E. Mingione (eds) *Beyond Employment: Gender, Household and Subsistence*, Oxford: Blackwell.

Morris, L. (1985) 'Renegotiation of the domestic division of labour in the context of redundancy', in B. Roberts, R. Finnegan, and D. Gallie (eds) *New Approaches to Economic Life*, Manchester: Manchester University Press.

——(1987) 'Constraints on gender: the family wage, social security and the labour market', *Work, Employment and Society* 1 (1).

Oakley, A. (1974) *The Sociology of Housework*, London: Martin Robertson.

——(1976) *Housewife*, Harmondsworth: Penguin.

Pahl, J. (1983) 'The allocation of money and the structuring of inequality within marriage', *Sociological Review* 31 (2).

Pahl, R. E. (1984) *Divisions of Labour*, Oxford: Blackwell.

Pahl, R. E. and Wallace, C. (1985) 'Household work strategies in economic recession', in N. Redclift and E. Mingione (eds) *Beyond Employment: Gender, Household and Subsistence*, Oxford: Blackwell.

Phillips, A. (1983) *Hidden Hands: Women and Economic Policies*, London: Pluto Press.

Pilgrim Trust (1938) *Men Without Work*, Cambridge: Cambridge University Press.

171

Pleck, J. H. (1979) 'Men's family work: three perspectives and some new data', *The Family Co-ordinator* (Oct).

Pollert, A. (1981) *Girls, Wives, Factory Lives*, London: Macmillan.

Porter, M. (1982) 'Standing on the edge: working class wives and the world of work', in J. West (ed.) *Work, Women and the Labour Market*, London: Routledge & Kegan Paul.

Potter, T. (1987) *A Temporary Phenomenon*, Birmingham: West Midlands Low Pay Unit.

Purcell, K., Wood, S., Waton, A., and Allen, S. (eds) (1986) *The Changing Experience of Employment*, London: Macmillan.

Rapoport, R. and Rapoport, R. N. (1978) *Working Couples*, London: Routledge & Kegan Paul.

Redclift, N. (1985) 'The contested domain: gender, accumulation and the labour process', in N. Redclift and E. Mingione (eds) *Beyond Employment: Gender, Household and Subsistence*, Oxford: Blackwell.

Redclift, N. and Mingione, E. (eds) (1985) *Beyond Employment: Gender, Household and Subsistence*, Oxford: Blackwell.

Rhodes, J. (1986) 'Regional dimensions of economic decline', in R. Martin and B. Rowthorn (eds) *The Geography of De-industrialisation*, London: Macmillan.

Roberts, B., Finnegan, R., and Gallie, D. (eds) (1985) *New Approaches to Economic Life*, Manchester: Manchester University Press.

Robinson, J. P., Converse, P. E., and Szalai, A. (1972) 'Everyday life in twelve countries', in A. Szalai (ed.) *The Use of Time*, The Hague: Mouton.

Rose, R. (1983) *Getting by in Three Economies*, University of Strathclyde, Studies in Public Policy, no.110.

Rowthorn, B. (1986) 'De-industrialisation in Britain', in R. Martin and B. Rowthorn (eds) *The Geography of De-industrialisation*, London: Macmillan.

Sawhill, I. V. (1977) 'Economic perspectives on the family', in A. H. Amsden (ed.) *The Economics of Women and Work*, Harmondsworth: Penguin.

Seccombe, W. (1976) 'Domestic labour: a reply to critics', *New Left Review* 94.

Smith, J. (1984) 'The paradox of women's poverty: wage-earning women and economic transformation', *Signs* 10 (2).

Smith, S. (1986) *Britain's Shadow Economy*, Oxford: Oxford University Press.

Stone, I. and Stevens, J. (1985) *Economic Restructuring and Employment Change on Wearside*, Sunderland Polytechnic EDU for EEC/ Borough of Sunderland.

——(1985/6) 'Employment on Wearside: trends and prospects', *Northern Economic Review* (Winter) 12.

Stromsheim, G. (1982) 'Part-time work as a labour Market phenomenon', in K. Hvidtfelt, K. Jorgensen, and R. Neilsen (eds) *Strategies for Integrating Women into the Labour Market*, Copenhagen: Women's Research Centre in Social Sciences.

Stubbs, C. and Wheelock, J. (1989) 'Gender and the Wearside local economy', *Northern Economic Review*, (Spring) 17.

Szalai, A. (1972) *The Use of Time*, The Hague: Mouton.
Tolson, A. (1977) *The Limits of Masculinity*, London: Tavistock.
Trew, K. and Kilpatrick, R. (1984) *The Daily Life of the Unemployed*, Dept. of Psychology, Queen's University, Belfast.
Vanek, J. (1974) 'Time spent in housework', in A. H. Amsden (ed.) *The Economics of Women and Work*, Harmondsworth: Penguin.
Veblen, T. (1912) *The Theory of the Leisure Class*, London: Macmillan.
Voydanoff, P. (1987) *Work and Family Life*, London: Sage.
Wajcman, J. (1983) *Women in Control: Dilemmas of a Workers' Co-operative*, Milton Keynes: Open University Press.
West, J. (ed.) (1982) *Work, Women and the Labour Market*, London: Routledge & Kegan Paul.
Wheelock, J. (1984) 'Competition in the Marxist tradition', *Capital and Class*, (Winter) 21.
——(1986) *Unemployment, Gender Roles and Household Work Strategies on Wearside*, Sunderland Polytechnic EDU for EEC/ Borough of Sunderland.
Williams, H. and Charles, D. (1986) 'The electronics industry in the North East: growth or decline?' *Northern Economic Review* (Summer) 13.
Wilson, E. (1987) 'Thatcherism and women: after seven years', in Socialist Register.
Yeandle, S. (1984) *Women's Working Lives*, London: Tavistock.
Young, M. and Wilmott, P. (1973) *The Symmetrical Family: A Study of Work and Leisure in the London Region*, London: Routledge & Kegan Paul.

Index